# *Leavetaking*

## WHEN AND HOW TO SAY GOODBYE

**by
Mortimer R. Feinberg, Ph.D.
Gloria Feinberg
John J. Tarrant**

GINN PRESS *Lexington, Massachusetts*

PUBLISHED BY GINN PRESS
191 SPRING STREET
LEXINGTON, MASSACHUSETTS 02173
ORIGINALLY PUBLISHED BY SIMON AND SCHUSTER

DESIGNED BY IRVING PERKINS
MANUFACTURED IN THE UNITED STATES OF AMERICA

LIBRARY OF CONGRESS CATALOGING IN PUBLICATION DATA

FEINBERG, MORTIMER R.

LEAVETAKING
    WHEN AND HOW TO SAY GOODBYE.

    INCLUDES INDEX.
    1. SEPARATION (PSYCHOLOGY)    I. FEINBERG, GLORIA, JOINT
AUTHOR.    II. TARRANT, JOHN H., JOINT AUTHOR
III. TITLE.
BF575.G7T37    155.9'2    78-1887
ISBN 0-536-05283-2

# Contents

# *Leavetaking*
### WHEN AND HOW TO SAY GOODBYE

# *1* TO LIVE IS TO SAY GOODBYE

LEAVETAKING IS the universal experience. From birth to death we face a continuum of partings. How well we handle leavetaking determines to a considerable extent whether we are happy or unhappy, integrated or fragmented.

Leavetaking is essential to growth. As we move into maturity—and beyond—we part from people, places, things, states of life. We must do this, or we do not grow.

But the process is often painful. We cling to relationships longer than we should. We are shocked when we are taken leave of. Our resistance to the change that leavetaking brings compels us to maintain associations that we should have outgrown, and makes us terribly vulnerable to the pain of rejection when an association is broken off. Sometimes we swing to the other extreme and sever relationships that we should have kept. Sometimes we take leave when we should but do it in ways that hurt ourselves and others.

As we look at life we can recognize the major leavetaking events.

*Birth.* The leaving of the womb. Physicians are increasingly coming to recognize the traumatic potentialities of this first episode in life, and they are experimenting with methods to reduce the shock—softer lights in the OB rooms, gentler handling, no more sharp slap on the buttocks.

*Weaning.* The handling of the transition from the oral and then the anal phase. Recent findings disclose that moving out of these stages involves a distinct form of leavetaking. The infant, for example, must take leave of its own feces; and some never really manage to accomplish this separation.

*School.* The first day, as many parents learn, can be very difficult. What is not as widely acknowledged is that the problems involved in leaving home to go to school cannot all be passed over as normal, and that this early leavetaking can hurt, not just temporarily, but for all of life.

*Overnight.* Darkness brings its special fears to a child. The first overnight stay away from home is a necessary leavetaking. It is not invariably managed well by parents (and here our culture places the principal burden on the mother).

*The first loss of a loved object.* It may be a relative or a friend. It may be a pet. It may even be an inanimate object —a toy. Because the object may be trivial, parents are often unaware of the pain the child feels when the object is lost.

*Longer leavetaking.* The growing child leaves for college, a temporary job, the service, or, more and more, just a trip. The process at this stage still envisions a return, but it is apt to be the last return. This leavetaking is one of the critical nexuses. It may be harder on the parent than on the child.

*The departure into the world.* One of the most perilous of leavetakings, particularly when the break is not clean, or when it is endlessly delayed, or when it does not happen at all. The child-adult does not go—or goes, leaving behind a parent or parents who display the symptoms of the "empty nest" syndrome.

*Breakup of the first love affair.* Though alliances may be entered casually, the ending of them may be not only messy but sometimes traumatic. The young eschew "hypocrisy." They will not buy the old rules. But they adopt the code of "cool"; and playing it cool can mask, but not heal, deep wounds.

*Marriage or its equivalent.* Commitment to a mate means taking leave of what is often seen in retrospect as carefree youth. The courts bulge with broken marriages in which one or both partners failed to say the necessary goodbyes to the past.

*Moving.* We put down roots, whether we realize it or not and whether we like the soil or not. Relocation can be traumatic. In the frequent cases in which the man is transferred by his company, the problem may be far less acute for him than for his wife and children.

*Leaving the job.* The job is a lot more than a means of making money. We become involved with the occupation, the workplace, and the people. These ties keep many people in jobs long after they should have resigned. However, when an individual is fired, the results are often shattering.

*Divorce or its equivalent.* Surviving the loss of a love— and of love itself, or its memory—is a challenge that defeats a great many of us. Here is a nexus replete with potentialities of bitterness, pain, despair and collapse.

*The deaths of friends and relatives.* We see our own end foreshadowed. We know how we *should* feel, and we are guilty for not feeling that way. Often we have too much self-pity and insufficient real grief.

*The fading of good health.* People fear the trip to the doctor. It may mean the realization of their fears. At some point we must all say goodbye to the physical beings that once we were. The point of leavetaking may be a serious illness, a general feeling of decline, an ebbing of sexual potency. The goodbye to good health is a hard leavetaking.

*Retirement.* In our culture retirement is not the entering of a new phase. It is relegation, if not to a "retirement home," at least to a role that is usually awkward, never welcomed.

*Death.* The final goodbye, the culmination of all the leavetakings.

The most obvious thing about leavetaking is that it is a universal experience no one can avoid.

Whether the leavetaking is voluntary or involuntary, the psychic mechanisms work the same. The person who breaks off a relationship often suffers more heavily than the one who is left, although the initial pain is greater for the latter individual.

In most leavetaking situations there is an active participant and a passive one. One person takes leave, the other is left. But volition is no over-all protection against the trauma of leavetaking. True, the active participant has the advantage of forethought and preparation, but the pain is shared. The person who is suddenly left feels rage, fear and bereavement. The person who has broken off the relationship feels guilt, self-hatred and bereavement.

Leavetaking fosters dangerous misapprehensions. The leave that seems to have been taken turns out to be a make-believe parting. The breaking-off may appear to have been successful, with no damage to either person, but in fact there is lasting damage. And, significantly, the leave that is not taken often has more harmful effects than the leave that is taken. Moreover, trivial leavetakings can be more difficult and painful than momentous ones.

Leavetaking is never an unalloyed joy. There is a "Catch-22" factor. Any time we begin to feel extremely happy about a parting, another element of the personality goes into action to adulterate this happiness with guilt and fear.

The effects of badly handled leavetaking are cumulative. The child who has experienced painful, anxious separation grows into the adult who clings beyond reason to every relationship or who tries never to form any relationship at all. And yet leavetaking is a necessary element of life. Parting must accompany growth. Without leavetaking we cannot mature. A healthy, developing life will show a pattern of changing relationships. Old relationships phase into new ones, which are more appropriate and need-satisfying. The general trend is away from the relationship that emphasizes *dependency* (an infant is all-dependent) toward attachment or association that provides mutual pleasures and satisfactions. The mature individual is not heavily dependent on others, but he does not try to deny that he must be dependent in some degree.

These observations raise certain questions:

How much pain is too much?

What is the equation between immediate distress of parting and long-term psychic damage?

When should one initiate a leavetaking?

How can one detect the signs that leavetaking is imminent?

Is it possible to prepare for parting so that ultimate trauma is reduced or obviated?

How does one cope with an unexpected and devastating loss?

Are there ways in which inner resources and protective mechanisms can be developed to prepare the individual for any difficult leavetaking, no matter what particular form it may take?

In sum, can we cope with leavetaking?

Leavetaking cannot be avoided, but it can be handled in ways that reduce trauma and foster growth. Before moving on to discuss specific safeguards and strategies, it is important that we consider more fully the role that leavetaking plays in our lives and the pitfalls that endanger each parting.

# *II* LEAVETAKING IN OUR CULTURE

CERTAIN HISTORIANS and philosophers are forever making connections between seemingly disparate entities—for example, associating the introduction of counterpoint in music with the invention of double-entry bookkeeping. This can be overdone, but there are undeniably more connections in our world than we sometimes think there are.

Today most developments seem calculated to increase the incidence of leavetaking. We are immeasurably more mobile than our forefathers. The Women's Liberation Movement gives structure and sanction to the breaking of traditional ties. Would the divorce rate be as high as it is if it were not for the development of convenience foods? Or does the cause-effect mechanism—if it applies at all—work the other way round?

Whatever the basic truth—and who can ever fathom it?—society today emphasizes leavetaking. The high marks are assigned to the individual who plunges into change, who strikes out on his own. It is the time of "split chic." Popular songs—for example, "Fifty Ways to Leave Your Lover"—reflect this feeling. The person who prefers to maintain existing associations is looked upon as unadventurous and somehow lacking in the stuff of heroism. The leavetaker as hero is a commonplace of our society. As a result, many more people are impelled into leavetaking than would, or should, undertake it on their own.

But parting has always been more intriguing than staying. Leavetaking is woven into our culture. The towering classics are about leavetaking. Homer's *Odyssey* offers archetypes that we may recognize today. Odysseus is the chronic leavetaker. He must always be on the move, always saying goodbye, no matter what the cost. The cost seems always to be paid by others, never by himself. From relationship to relationship he sails away. The adventures are functions of the drive to take leave. At last, after years of wandering, he comes to rest at home in Ithaca. Is he truly at rest? We cannot believe that he is. More recent writers tell us the story of his continued goodbyes. Kazantzakis tells of Odysseus' further wayfarings, through the islands of Greece, down the length of Africa, to his death amid the ice floes near the South Pole.* Tennyson writes of the hero's growing restlessness in Ithaca and his resumed travels: "For my purpose holds to sail beyond the sunset, and the baths of western stars, until I die."

Joyce's *Ulysses* gives us a different type of leavetaker. Bloom is the wanderer who cannot say goodbye to the past—to his youth, to departed friends, to his dead son.

Homer's Odysseus offers one more aspect of the chronic leavetaker. The wanderer seems never to be affected, let alone scarred, by his continued goodbyes. But then, at the end, there is the explosion, the orgy of anger and blood, in which the wily sophisticate destroys Penelope's suitors.

There are other archetypes in Homer. There is the nymph

* Nikos Kazantzakis, *The Odyssey: A Modern Sequel* (New York: Simon and Schuster, 1958).

Calypso. At the beginning of the poem Odysseus is with her on the island of Ogygia. Calypso is one of the "nicest" characters in all mythology. She has saved Odysseus from death. She loves him selflessly. She has given him, and is willing to give him, everything. She is a source of unending sexual variety and pleasure. She weaves him fine clothes with her golden shuttle. She has created a fantastic bower, a fragrant grove replete with blossoms and fountains. She feeds him on nectar and ambrosia. She is ready to bestow immortality on him, or she is willing to abandon her own godhood, if only he will stay. "In every other way except in giving him his freedom," writes Edith Hamilton, "she overwhelmed him with kindness; all that she had was at his disposal."*

However, nothing will do Odysseus but that he must leave her. In the end he resorts to a classic technique—employing a third person. Through the intervention of Athena, Zeus is persuaded to send Hermes to talk with Calypso. Hermes uses a combination of persuasion and threat on the unhappy nymph, and at last she agrees to let Odysseus go.

Ariadne is like Calypso. The daughter of Minos, she falls in love with Theseus. She helps Theseus to find his way through the labyrinth and kill the Minotaur. She relies on Theseus' promise that he will take her to Athens and marry her. They get as far as the island of Naxos, where Theseus employs a more direct technique than Odysseus. He simply sails away, abandoning her. Ariadne pines, longing for death, until she is awakened to life by the god Dionysus. Did Dionysus stay with her? They remained married, but Dionysus was often gone, spreading his orgiastic doctrine throughout the world. Calypsos and Ariadnes often seem to wind up with characters like Dionysus.

Circe did not react to leavetaking like Calypso. Circe is a destroyer. She cannot say goodbye; she destroys instead. She

---

* Edith Hamilton, *Mythology* (Boston: Little, Brown, 1942).

loved Glaucus, but lost him to Scylla; so she changed Scylla into a horrible monster.

Circe bids many hello on her island of Aeaea but few goodbye. When the seafaring men stop there she turns them into animals rather than suffer them to depart from her. She changes Odysseus' crew into pigs, keeps them in a sty, feeds them acorns. Odysseus—again with the help of Hermes— outwits her. Reluctantly she turns the pigs back into men.

Odysseus, the eternal leavetaker; Calypso, always fated to be left; Circe, who destroys before she will say goodbye—all types whom we meet today.

The movies, and the scenes in movies, that we remember the best are frequently about leavetaking: Rhett Butler saying goodbye to Scarlett, and Scarlett not accepting it, consoling herself that "tomorrow will be another day"; Shane riding away from the little boy at the fadeout; Dorothy bidding farewell to the Cowardly Lion, the Scarecrow and the Tin Man as she prepares to leave the Land of Oz.

A movie that has achieved enduring and monumental fame is *Grand Illusion*. Jean Renoir's great work was released in 1937 and is still a favorite at festivals throughout the world.

*Grand Illusion* is leavetaking in a variety of forms. On the surface it is about World War I, but there is no fighting. The action concerns Frenchmen who are captives of the Germans. There are four principal characters, each representing a type. Von Rauffenstein (Erich von Stroheim) is the German commandant. Rauffenstein is a Prussian aristocrat, imbued with the old ways, scornful of a changing world. De Boeldieu, the senior French officer, is also an aristocrat, with lineage as long and honorable as that of Rauffenstein. Marechal (Jean Gabin) represents the vigorous, earthy French middle class. Rosenthal is a rich Frenchman; he is also a Jew.

Rauffenstein seeks the friendship and understanding of Boeldieu in alliance against the upstart representatives of alien classes and an unwelcome new order. But unlike the

German, Boeldieu knows his day is past. He is willing to say his goodbyes to the world he once knew. As a ruse to cover the escape of others, Boeldieu makes a spectacular run for it across the prison roof, and Rauffenstein, in psychic agony, shoots him down.

Marechal and Rosenthal escape together. Together they must make their way across Germany. The friction between them grows. At last Marechal leaves his companion, screaming, "You know what you are to me? A ball and chain! I always hated Jews!" But Marechal comes back.

Almost spent, the two take refuge on a remote German farm. The German farm woman, whose husband has left her for the war, hides them, feeds them, clothes them. Marechal makes love to her. He finds that for the first time in his life he is happy, living with the German woman, running the farm. But with the coming of spring Marechal decides that he must move on, and Rosenthal must go with him. Marechal tells the woman he will come back. Her face conveys her suffering and her resignation to the knowledge that he will not come back.

Marechal and Rosenthal, floundering through the Alpine snow, try desperately for the Swiss border. They are spotted by a German patrol. The soldiers take aim. Then the corporal orders, "Don't shoot!" The soldiers lower their guns. The Frenchmen are across the border. The final long shot shows them as specks in the snow, stumbling away from the viewer.

*Grand Illusion* is about people taking leave of each other in spite of self-interest, friendship or love; about people taking leave of stages of life; and about the farewell to life itself. As the picture fades from the screen we are silent and pensive, thinking of our own goodbyes.

The tough private-eye detective story is a staple of American —and, by extension, British and European—popular fiction. This genre is based to a considerable extent on the lacerating effects of leavetaking.

Raymond Chandler, who picked up the torch from the hands of Dashiell Hammett, is celebrated as a master of hard-boiled realism. Chandler's specialty, in fact, is soft-boiled romanticism. His stories are first-person chronicles told by the detective Philip Marlowe. Marlowe wanders through a series of adventures. Most of any Chandler book, however, consists less of action than of conversation between Marlowe and the hustlers, losers and thugs whom he confronts. These episodes are interspersed with Marlowe's soliloquies. Throughout, the detective's thoughts are suffused with self-pity strained through cynicism.

Why is Marlowe sorry for himself? He is always saying goodbye but never quite bringing it off. He meets people, mostly bad, some good. If they live (and people who meet Philip Marlowe have a high mortality rate) he breaks off relations with them. But he yearns with all the fervor of Goethe's young Werther, and is always drifting back toward the past, toward the people he once knew, toward his own youth and careless strength; but he knows he can never really go back.

Chandler's last full-scale novel is *The Long Goodbye*. It has flaws as a detective story, but it is a powerful book. *The Long Goodbye,* beginning with the title, is about leavetaking. Some of the characters say goodbye to other characters, but the break is never clean. Others want to say goodbye but can't, and are driven to violence. The murderer kills because she was once in love with someone and the effective leavetaking was never made. Marlowe's melancholy is deepened by his sense of the loss of his own more vigorous yesterday. Insulted by a gangster, he hauls himself wearily to his feet and punches the thug in the belly, reflecting all the while on the toll paid to the passing years. Toward the end, one of the two women he ever loved comes into his life again. He sleeps with her. This is momentous. The sexy, amoral Marlowe does not usually engage in sex, despite the opportunities. This episode is a one-night stand. She goes, and Marlowe is left with the burden of one more botched goodbye.

Raymond Chandler's most celebrated successor, Ross Macdonald, writes private-eye novels that weave tapestries of separation, loss and pain. Nothing is ever finished in a Macdonald book. The pattern is always the same. The detective, Lew Archer, takes on a chase that presents the normal (for this milieu) aspects of violence, lust and greed. Inevitably he follows the skein back into the past, digging up the bodies, literally and figuratively. People who have been thought dead for many years return to life. Relationships broken off decades ago are renewed, to dismal and sinister purpose. The thread stretches back as far as five generations. In the end, the designation of an actual culprit is almost insignificant, so monumental are the piles of shards from the past which surround it.

These books, ostensibly about murder, are really about leavetaking. They evoke the sadness and fear of parting. In this, rather than in the plotting, characterization or narrative, they call to something in the reader.

Note the names that these authors give to their detectives. "Marlowe" is not a commonplace name for anyone, let alone a policeman. The only Marlowe most of us have heard of is the Elizabethan poet. Raymond Chandler received a public school education in England. His father deserted his mother. They were forced to move to California. Chandler lost his job as an oil company executive. Then he turned to writing. Marlowe was born. Macdonald acknowledges his debt to the past by naming his detective after Miles Archer, Sam Spade's partner in the seminal private-eye fiction of Dashiell Hammett.

There is a whole literature in which the thrust is not death or the enjoyment of a puzzle's unraveling; it is the ever-present past and the fear of goodbye.

Our attitudes toward leavetaking reveal themselves even in the language we use in leavetaking situations. How often do we say *"Goodbye"*? Not often; "goodbye" has come to connote finality. Even when the parting is permanent we resort to words that imply that it is temporary. We say "So long," "See you again," "We'll get together again" (one interesting variation, "Let's have lunch sometime"), "Hasta luego," "Auf wiedersehen," "A rivederci," "Au revoir."

Some of us find it difficult to leave a party. We linger on the doorstep unable to say a final goodbye. (Some researchers believe that there is an interesting psychological dynamic at work in this situation. They infer that the lingering leavetaker never received satisfaction at the party, so he stays on, hoping that at the end something will happen to compensate for all that was missing earlier in the evening.)

The preacher at the funeral service intones, "He is not dead; he only sleepeth." When one person says something that appears to recognize finality—"Well, I guess this is it"—the other person will hasten to utter words of denial—"Oh, we'll be getting together again." This happens even when the two are merely casual acquaintances and the parting involves little if any pain. We speak the ritual words that convey the illusion that no parting is final or even of any great importance. Our actions and our language are a generally accepted denial of the fact of goodbye.

As if the pain of leavetaking were not enough on its own, we have to cope with the rules of a society that dictate a hierarchy of responses to grief. When we react in ways that run counter to that established hierarchy, we are in trouble.

An eighteen-year-old boy writes to Ann Landers (New York *Daily News*, November 4, 1976). He feels guilty because he did not shed a tear at his grandmother's funeral, but when his cat died he could not stop crying.

The fact that you feel worse about parting from a "casual" relationship or a "trivial" thing than from an association that is conventionally supposed to be important does not make you a bad or inadequate person. No one really understands grief. We cannot control many of the attachments we make.

What is small to one individual is big to another. Furthermore, grief does not always come in a convenient package immediately upon the heels of a loss. Its resonances may become overwhelming at a later time. We suffer what would appear to be a major loss; we seem to feel nothing. Six months later we lose something that seems far less significant and we are shattered. The second leavetaking has opened the floodgate that dammed up full response to the first.

Ned H. Kassem writes of a young girl whose right arm had been amputated after the discovery of bone cancer. She attended the funeral of her grandfather, whom she had not known at all well. She began to cry bitterly and was unable to stop. It became clear that she was weeping for her lost arm. She did not cry at home because it made her parents sad. "It felt so good to have an *excuse to cry,*" she said (emphasis added).*

We all need to cry. The trouble is that we have to find an excuse to cry.

There has not been much attention paid to leavetaking as a shaping factor in life. The psychological literature discusses "separation anxiety" from time to time. The most familiar application is to children. While the existence of separation anxiety in adults is acknowledged, it is less frequently studied.

For the most part, the traumatic effects of leavetaking, actual or anticipated, have been discussed in the context of other and more familiar psychological concepts. A child screams and becomes hysterical during the first day at school. A young man breaks up with his girl and becomes impotent. A wife who moves with her husband to a new job location begins to drink heavily and pick up men at a nearby bar. A mother whose children have left the house eats herself into gargantuan obesity. A formerly healthy man, suffering a mild heart attack, goes into a severe and prolonged depression. A

---

* Ned H. Kassem, in Vanderlyn R. Pine *et al.,* eds., *Acute Grief and the Funeral* (Springfield, Ill.: Thomas, 1975).

daughter whose mother has just died erupts in a paroxysm of guilt and rage.

We propose to consider such episodes from the viewpoint of their similar elements. A common threat runs through all. Parting—from loved ones, or places, or things, or states of life—may in many cases be merely the mechanism that triggers a reaction whose roots lie in the neurotic components of one's personality. But considerable study shows that the leavetaking itself may be more than the trigger; it may be the causative agent.

There is an even more important reason for us to look at the totality of leavetaking in life. To live satisfactory lives we must grow. All of us grow physically; we accept as truth the proposition that we must grow intellectually and emotionally as well. From the days of Freud on down, new concepts have been greeted with the criticism that they are applicable only within a particular culture, that they lack universality. Freud's critics attack his precepts as applying only to middle-class individuals (predominantly male) who are steeped in what is loosely called "Western culture."

The urge toward growth and the acceptance of the need to grow would seem to be about as universal as a concept can be. Cultures of today and two thousand years ago—primitive and advanced—acknowledge the "growth imperative." Advancement toward maturity is a recognized essential throughout the world and throughout history. Rites of passage— ritualizations of growth from one phase of life into another— abound in society, from the scarring of the face of the adolescent in New Guinea to the Bar Mitzvah of a boy in Shaker Heights. We know we have to grow. But growing means saying goodbye.

For most of us saying goodbye is not easy. We cling—to people, to the past. A twenty-two-year-old comes home. He has been graduated from college. He has traveled the country on his own. It is time for him to get a job. On his first night home he buys five airplane models at a hobby shop and for the next several days occupies himself with an activity he last engaged in at the age of twelve. His parents' reaction: he is lazy, he is stalling. The boys wants to grow. He knows it is expected of him. But he finds it awfully hard to take leave of the whole of his life up till now.

When we know when to say goodbye, and act on it, we grow. We don't always know when to say goodbye. Or we do know, but we don't want to; and we procrastinate until the leavetaking happens unexpectedly, involuntarily, clumsily, and traumatically. Some of us never take our leave at the right time; a few of us never really take it at all. Some of us are always saying goodbye, or wishing we could say goodbye, or resenting every moment that must pass until we can say goodbye. There is pain in all of this, and lasting damage in a lot of it.

A view of life as a series of leavetakings may not provide us with the one final answer. It can, however, give us a great many partial answers that help us to move through life. The biggest of these answers is understanding. When we understand the nature of leavetaking, and accept it as an integral part of existence—rather than a recurring difficulty that can somehow be avoided—we may form a useful idea of the ways in which the leavetakings of the past have affected us. We will, too, be able to anticipate the partings ahead and prepare for them.

Understanding is one essential in dealing with the universal fact of leavetaking. By seeing it as a distinct factor of life we gain the kind of insight that is a prerequisite for control of our fate and progress toward maturity. There is another, important area into which a discussion of the topic can take us. This is "what to do" as opposed to "what is happening." There are ways to handle leavetaking and the pain it causes, ways to minimize the harmful effects on ourselves and on others. There are methods of determining the right time to say goodbye. There are techniques for handling the difficult act. And there are methods by which we can minimize the trauma of partings that have happened to us and of building our resistance to the hurtful consequences of the next parting we will have to face.

There are two kinds of losses in bereavement, role loss and object loss. Regina Flesch illustrates this with the example of the mother whose child dies. "Typically," says Dr. Flesch, "the bereaved mother starts to follow her old routines, but fails to carry them through to completion. The routines are no longer purposeful because the person who gave them meaning is no longer among the living."*

She grieves for the child, the object. But she has also lost her role as a mother. We become attached to habits and routines just as we do to people. When the meaning is removed from the routine, we don't know what to do. We are like fish out of water. And it happens in other kinds of leavetaking, not just death. The children go away from home. A marriage breaks up. We lose a job. We have to move to another location.

Object loss is apt to be the first of the two elements that we feel. We think with nostalgic longing about the person or thing that has gone out of our lives. We are sentimental. We pine. But object loss soon becomes mixed with role loss. We still miss what is gone, but we begin to think, too, about the effect of the loss on our functioning. We become aware of all of the ways in which the routine of our lives has been geared to what is no longer with us. We realize, more or less, the current pointlessness of that routine, but we have nothing with which to replace it. We ask, "What do I do now?"

Object loss is sentimental longing; role loss is situational anxiety. When the process of grieving works normally, we

* Regina Flesch, in *ibid.*

tend to phase from sentimental longing into situational anxiety. The memory of the departed object does not disappear, but it grows dimmer. The concern about the next steps to be taken becomes, in turn, sharper. This is healthy progress; situational anxiety, if it is not distorted into morbidity, is a positive reaction. It focuses on reality. It concerns itself with "real world" decisions. It sets the stage for growth into the next phase of life.

Many people involved in leavetaking permit the object-loss aspect to dominate the process. They repress the aspects of role loss. Sometimes they do this because they think that any consideration of practicalities is a disservice to the departed object. Sometimes they do it because they cannot face up to the hard decisions required by realignment with the real world.

So they do not work on solving the situational problems. They stick to the old routine and look for another object around which these routines can orbit. The idea is to continue the former practices, even though there is a hole at the center, and to fill that hole as quickly as possible with an object that resembles as closely as possible that which has been lost. This is not a winning proposition, but there is a universal tendency to bet on it. That is one of the things that make singles bars so popular and at the same time so tragic.

TOWARD AN UNDERSTANDING
OF LEAVETAKING

THE NATURAL PROGRESSION of healing flows from absorption
with object loss to consideration of role loss—from sentimental reaction to situational concern. We go through the
process of denying, being angry, missing, grieving, feeling
guilty. Eventually, if we are to survive and grow, we must
come to the stage at which we focus on those things we *can*
do something about.

There is always more or less pain involved in any substantial
parting. However, *the pain is not the trauma.* The immediate
distress is more likely to be a necessary psychic mechanism
that reduces the longer-range damage.

The trauma associated with leavetaking takes various forms.
The individual may become mildly or deeply neurotic or
even psychotic. There may be depression (sometimes interspersed with wild upward swings of euphoria), anger, anxiety,
guilt. A person scarred by a parting may drink heavily, worry

to excess, become promiscuous. There are other effects: for example, a mother may get fat after her children leave. Her obesity is an attempt to deny the fact of leavetaking.

At any given time most people are involved in a stage of leavetaking. Since life comprises multiple associations, an individual may be affected by different phases of parting with relation to various relationships. For example, let's look at one family.

Alice B. is forty-four. Her husband, George, was transferred from Georgia to the Chicago office three years ago. Alice has tried to get used to living in Winnetka. They have a nice house, George moved to a better job. But Alice had lived her whole life in Atlanta. She can't get used to the new place.

George B. is forty-six. When the transfer came he welcomed it; more money, more authority. But the Chicago office is different from the one in Atlanta. The pace is faster. The office politics are tougher. Last week George learned of a meeting to which he was not invited; he should have been invited to it. There are other things. He walked into his boss's office and found his boss with the president of the company. They stopped talking and looked at George with strained smiles. There is a younger man, aggressive ("pushy," George thinks) and ambitious. George thought he was set for life. Now he is not so sure. Could they fire him? If it happens, what will he do?

Donald B., twenty-two. He had been at Chapel Hill. For a year Donald lived there with Kate. Then Kate walked out on him. Since then Donald has been impotent. He is heavily on drugs. He has dropped out of school.

Harold B., sixty-nine. He has been retired for four years. His son George and daughter-in-law Alice used to be very close. Even after they moved away they used to phone, and he visited them or they visited him six times in two years. Harold's wife died a year ago. He has not been able to get over it. He has not seen George and Alice since the funeral.

And the other day he felt a sharp, agonizing pain in his chest. Harold B. used to boast that he was never sick a day in his life. He is afraid to go to the doctor.

Each of these people is suffering the trauma of leavetaking. Their problems differ in detail, but they are alike in that they involve object loss—the loss of the cherished or familiar person, thing or condition—and role loss—the termination of an important part that one plays in life.

The general thrust of the strategies outlined in this book is to enable leavetaker and leavetaken to ride out the storm of object loss—the denial, the rage, the guilt, the loneliness —and then to cope with the element of the problem that is more important and more manageable: role loss.

But we are not talking merely of survival. The opposite of role loss is *role gain*. A healthy maturing process involves the shedding of roles that are no longer appropriate and the assumption of new roles that are commensurate with growth. To grow we must do more than just passively endure the breaking off of relationships. We have to be able to anticipate leavetakings and prepare to handle them. We have to be able to replace bygone associations with new ones that satisfy our needs. And, beyond this, we must be prepared to take the initiative, breaking old relationships and moving into new ones with the least pain and greatest benefit to all who are involved.

It can be done. The first step is a better understanding of leavetaking and the ways in which it shapes life.

Leavetaking assumes many forms. However, we can identify those life events that carry the highest potential for psychic damage. They begin at birth and end at death. They include the departure of children from the home, the breakup of the marriage, the leaving of one's community, parting, abruptly or gradually, from one's occupation, the aging of parents.

Our success or failure in coping with one leavetaking event influences our ability to handle the next event. However, every crisis of parting offers the opportunity to make a better accommodation with change if we are willing to open ourselves to the pain of the past and make the objective decisions that will control the future.

Let's begin in childhood. Freud offered two propositions that are now widely accepted. The first is that many forms of psychiatric disorder stem from the inability of a person to make and maintain affectional bonds with other people. The second is that the patterns on which the adult's affectional bonds are shaped have been determined to a significant extent by events in his childhood, notably his relationship with his mother. (In this context, as in others throughout the book, the words "him" and "his" refer to both males and females.)

Affectional bonding is no recent evolutionary development. It is built into us through biological inheritance. Many animals develop strong and persistent bonds between one individual and another. The most persistent bond is usually that between mother and young. This is true in man as in the lower animals. Many of the most intense of our emotions arise during the formation, the maintenance, the disruption and the renewal of affectional bonds. And disruption of such ties can have the most traumatic effects.

We fall in and out of love. We make friends and lose them. We get married and we get divorced. People die. The breaking of affectional bonds is as prevalent in life as their formation.

For a long time—until the mid-1950s—orthodox psychiatric thinking held that bonds were developed between human beings because the individual had needs that could be met only through the formation of such attachments. This theory postulated two kinds of drives, primary and secondary. We need food and sex: that's primary. We need dependence: that's secondary. (Anna Freud called this a "cupboard love" theory of human relations.)

Within the last twenty years we have been considering a

great volume of evidence indicating that strong bonds can develop between individuals without any rewards being given or drives being met. In his first studies of imprinting, Konrad Lorenz demonstrated that in certain species of birds strong bonds are formed with a mother figure without reference to the need for food. All it takes is exposure to the mother figure. In one related experiment, newly hatched ducklings were induced to regard a football as the mother figure and to act toward this object in every way that the bird would act toward its mother. Dr. Harry Harlow demonstrated that a young monkey will cling to a figure that is soft even though it provides no food, and he will reject a dummy that feeds him but is not soft. The infant seems to need to be close to *some* object. Its reasons depend partly on such things as movement, sound and texture, and partly on familiarity.

This is attachment behavior. Its counterpart is caretaking behavior, seen most notably in mothers, but also in fathers and, in some species, in the attitude of any dominant animal toward a subordinate one.

During the course of human life we expect an individual to engage first in attachment behavior, then in heterosexual pair formation, and then in caretaking behavior, while forming a few other affectional bonds throughout the process.

We are learning that attachment behavior is not only the first of these forms of development but the most influential. The ways in which attachment behavior operates during a person's childhood sets a pattern that deeply influences the ways in which his sexual behavior and caretaking behavior—indeed his entire approach to the formation of attachments—will take place through life.

So the mother-child relationship casts its shadow forward for a lifetime. In a general way we all know this. The importance of the child-mother relationship has become a truism and something of a joke. References to it among adults range from pious reverence to caustic denigration. Ohio State football coach Woody Hayes once assured an audience in all seriousness that one of the reasons for the continuing success of his teams was that Ohio State quarterbacks had always had good relationships with their mothers. At the other end of the scale, Philip Roth drew the archetype of the shrewish Jewish mother in *Portnoy's Complaint* (with the implied corollary that you don't have to be Jewish to be or have a "Jewish mother").

Nevertheless, in beginning to understand our present approach to attachment, and in particular to the breaking of attachment involved in leavetaking, we do well to journey back toward childhood.

In humans, attachment behavior is usually at its most striking during the second and third year of life. This is when the child most wants to be within sight or sound of a mother figure. But even at this stage there should be offsetting influences. Erik Erikson observes that this is the point at which the infant must begin to develop a sense of autonomy as an alternative to "meaningless and arbitrary experiences of shame and early doubt." If a child exhibits no behavior except mother attachment, he will not develop normally. Normally, he explores, he investigates, he exercises his curiosity, he tries things out, he plays with other children. So exploration and attachment lead in different directions. However, they are closely linked. A child will muster up the courage to explore only when he is sure that the mother figure is close at hand and easily accessible. In a sense, the exploring child is engaging in what we call elsewhere in this book "dry-run" leavetaking. He is like an astronaut taking a spacewalk while still attached to the mother ship through the umbilicals.

As the child grows older he will become more adventurous. Increasingly lengthy spells away from the mother become a matter of course, but exploration still bears a relationship to the reassurance that mother is there if you need her. And it is important to note that this need is not necessarily predicated on the conventional picture of a "good" mother, one who is always sympathetic, ministering to hurts, cooing words or endearment. A "bad" mother is as necessary as a good one.

Attachment behavior does not cease when we grow out of childhood. When we are troubled or sick we seek the company of those we know and trust, and we are unhappy and anxious if they are not available. We are damaged when we must take leave of such figures. Attachment behavior is not regressive or childish; it is a normal part of human nature throughout life.

Attaching oneself to another person is not the same as depending on that person. Attachment and dependency are quite different concepts. We can be attached to our elderly parents but in no way dependent on them. We depend on the airline pilot while we are aloft, but we don't become attached to him.

In our society, dependency is something to be avoided. Conversely, we value attachment. We revere the independent, "self-made" figure who surmounts problems and makes his way through life without getting help from other people. We disapprove of the individual, independent though he may be, who does not form attachments. He is a "cold fish," an antisocial person.

One trouble with all this is that dependency and attachment do not, in practice, remain separate from each other. The child is attached to its mother. It is also dependent on its mother. The weaning process is supposed to reduce dependency but not attachment. It doesn't always work that way. Furthermore, when it does work that way, we don't always perceive the distinction between the two mechanisms.

A child grows toward maturity. Having reached the age of, say, fourteen, the child is inclined to strike out on his own. (His choice, says Erikson, lies between identity and role confusion.) His dependency on parents is diminished. He looks more toward his own developing resources. This is natural and proper. At the same time, his love for his mother—his attachment—remains in full force.

But it may be that the mother does not see it that way. She sees the slackening of the ties of dependence and assumes that the child's attachment is also waning. So she tries to maintain the close relationship by maintaining the bonds of dependency. She does not realize that the umbilical cord of dependency should properly shrivel and fall away and that, when it does, the cord of attachment can remain healthy. Indeed, strenuous efforts to keep up the ties of dependency can cause both dependency and attachment to die.

But not always. The parent may be successful in imposing the unnatural continuation of dependency. The result is bad for both parent and child. Each develops a warped view of relationship with others. The problem becomes most critical when the time comes to handle the leavetakings that are an integral part of life.

Regression stems not from attachment, but from excessive dependency. What happens is a psychic version of neoteny, a zoological phenomenon involving retention of juvenile characteristics in the adult. For example, the axolotl is a small salamander that lives in the water while in its larval stage. If the axolotl were to follow its normal life cycle it would lose its gills and grow into a land-dwelling adult. Often, however, this animal remains essentially in its juvenile form. It matures sexually while very young and breeds. It is still a larva, never having developed to full adulthood, and its offspring, in turn, remain larval, and breed the subsequent generation of infants, which also never entirely grow up.

Similarly, the world is full of people who look like adults and who possess the reproductive capacity but who have not outgrown their juvenile phase. They go through life prey to the same dependency needs and skewed attitudes toward leavetaking that they manifested when young, and they often influence their children to remain in the larval stage as well. One of the most significant characteristics of such lack of development is the retention in adult life of excessive separation anxiety.

Separation anxiety can be defined as the distress that accompanies loss or the danger of loss. The concept has been coming under increasing professional scrutiny in recent years, to a considerable extent as a result of the pioneering work of the British psychiatrist John Bowlby.

Bowlby describes the pattern of separation anxiety among young children in one of its most typical forms. The child develops an attachment to his mother. Then he is separated from her. At first he protests vigorously and tries by all means available to bring her back. Then he seems to despair of recovering her; nevertheless he remains preoccupied with her and vigilantly looks for her return. In the next phase the child seems to lose interest in his mother and to become emotionally detached from her. The mother comes back. For days, perhaps longer, the child insists on staying close to his mother, trying to follow her wherever she goes. At first he withholds his affection. Whenever he suspects that his mother may go away again he exhibits acute anxiety. However, if the period of separation has not been too prolonged the child does not remain detached indefinitely, and gradually his anxiety about losing her again is reduced.

As the child grows he becomes more able to handle the idea of separation. His cognitive (thinking) apparatus begins to develop. Separation may still evoke anxious emotions, but the capacity to think offsets these emotions, puts them in perspective, reinforces the rational view that separation is not calamity.

But the vestiges of the separation anxiety of childhood never disappear entirely. Throughout life we tend to be drawn toward persons, places and things that are familiar and to avoid those that are unfamiliar. Leavetaking always causes us a certain amount of distress. The ways in which we react to it and the degree of anxiety we feel about it are heavily influenced by our experiences as children.

When adults are asked to describe situations that frightened them as children, the memories they find most vivid are those connected with separation. We usually do not recall, for example, fear of death at an early age, but we do remember the anxiety and fear of leavetaking. Death gradually acquires its emotional significance through its connection with separation. Children's fairy tales do not dwell on death, but note how frequently they stress the theme of separation—abandonment by parents, the feeling of being alone in the dark and forbidding forest.

So one of the most significant elements of the maturing process is the increasing mastery of separation anxiety. We become skillful and resourceful. We develop confidence in our ability to handle strange situations. We learn that the unknown does not always mean danger. And yet few of us reach a point at which we are able to handle separation without at least a twinge of anxiety.

There is a school of thought that attaches lifelong significance to the shock of leavetaking at the moment when the baby emerges from the womb. The Austrian psychologist Otto Rank advanced this theory in 1924 in *The Trauma of Birth.* (Soon afterward Rank took leave of Freud because of Freud's disagreement with this proposition.)

The idea underlying this is that the leaving of the womb is a traumatic experience that stamps us with impressions about life that affect us as long as we live. These impressions are, on the whole, negative. We don't want to leave the warm comfort and safety of the womb and enter the unknown. The fear and shock of that moment have imprinted themselves on our subconscious.

Now this concept is edging back into fashion. For example, some people pay to do the following. They take off all their clothes, put on diving masks and nose clips, enter a vat of warm water, and then thrash around and scream.

These people are undergoing "rebirthing." They are pretending to be fetuses, suspended in the amniotic fluid within the womb, reliving their own births. Rebirthing is a concept being promoted by Theta, an organization founded by a former consultant to est, the galvanically successful self-realization company.

Some of those who undergo this therapy maintain that they can remember vividly the moment of birth and that it was horrible. They feel that the reliving of the experience helps them to get rid of their fears and live life more fully.

There is considerable question about the validity of the premise. There is question whether rebirthing has any permanent therapeutic effect beyond the momentary catharsis of the episode, and, if there are beneficial effects, whether they result from actual reduction of the effects of birth trauma or from some other combination of factors.

However, in discussing the problem of recovering from a traumatic leavetaking at any stage of life, it is worthwhile to draw upon some of the principles being used here.

The pain of leavetaking diminishes in intensity and duration, but we keep on getting flashbacks. The long-term effects may be guilt, fear, and anxiety. We try to recreate the past. We shy away from forming new relationships to replace those that have been broken.

While doing this we try to suppress the memory of the break itself. We are not altogether successful; we don't forget the abandonment of a loved one or the death of someone close. But we avoid thinking about the actual events of the leavetaking.

A form of rebirthing can be helpful. Let's say you are some time past a leavetaking that hurt you very much. Instead of fighting to suppress it, force yourself to relive it. Recall the details; this is what I saw that convinced me it was about to happen; this it what he said when it came to a crisis; these are the things I did to try to stave it off.

Remember your feelings of denial, of anger, and of shame for the things that you might have done. Then think about your fears at the time and your view of the future. Perhaps you could not envision life going on: "I want to die." You could not imagine that you would be able to cope. You thought the pain would never abate.

How much of that holds true today? Yes, you still hurt. You have problems adjusting. But life has gone on. The pain has diminished. There are resources available to you, whether you are calling on them or not.

The fact that you are able with any measure of success to think back on these things means something. It means that the healing process has been going forward without your knowing about it. Your mind is working. It has not been permanently impaired by the emotional fallout of the parting.

When you "rebirth" yourself after a severe breakage of an association, you will not come out feeling that things are even worse than you thought at the time. You are almost sure to conclude that the result, while bad, has not been quite as bad as you anticipated. And as you recall your emotions and the actions that gave rise to them, you will begin to identify the factors that are holding you back from making a full adjustment to what must come next.

Your "rebirth" can be the start of regeneration of your self-realizing faculties.

# *IV* THE ANGUISH OF THE EMPTY NEST

Children grow up and go away from home.

Except for death, this event is the most predictable of leave-takings. There is ample time to prepare for it. But some parents are not prepared when the moment comes. They try in various ways to keep their children from leaving. They become angry at children when they do leave. In extreme cases a parent will attempt to forestall the parting by reverting toward childhood and undertaking a futile effort to become contemporary with the children.

It's called the "empty nest" syndrome. We might more accurately term it the "empty heart."

Doris and Bob Calloway have always prided themselves on being good parents. They have read the books, gone to the meetings, taken an interest in their children. And it seems to have paid off. For example, Dick, their oldest, has always been a good boy and a joy to have around. In elementary school he was a serious, obedient, and winning child. In high school his schoolwork dropped off some, but the Calloways have tried to help. They have spent anxious hours with teachers and guidance counselors. They have been understanding and supportive with Dick. They have tried to walk the tightrope between too much and too little. They have not let Dick run free like some kids, but they have attempted to keep limitations to a sensible minimum. They could have afforded to give the boy a lot bigger allowance than they did. Many of the older kids in high school had their own cars; the Calloways have resisted Dick's pleas for wheels. They have made every effort to be modern about the drug question, going through miseries over the well-supported suspicion that Dick had at least tried pot, and being reassured when it did not seem that he was into anything harder. They have not tried to dictate their son's choice of friends, activities or future; they have offered guidance.

Up until three months before graduation the Calloways assumed that Dick would go on to college—the same college his father had attended. Then Dick detonated his bombshell. He did not want to go to college. What would he do? Well, bum around, go out west, see the country. Some friends were going to live in Colorado; maybe he'd try that. (*A hippie commune?* The Calloways blanched.)

To the Calloways the situation was dangerous. If they said "no" flatly, they feared that Dick would go anyway, and the consequences of such a parting were too much to bear.

At this point, though, the attitudes of the parents began to diverge. Bob Calloway started to talk about how maybe it was not such a bad thing for Dick to get off on his own for a while, lots of kids were doing it, things were different nowadays from when he and Doris were young, possibly something could be worked out so that Dick wasn't completely off on his own, and so forth.

Doris Calloway would have none of it. Her fears mounted.

Her attitude solidified. The veneer of the "with it" mother began to strip away. She insisted that under no circumstances was she willing to "lose" Dick. When Bob protested that such an arrangement was not necessarily losing the boy, Doris turned on her husband. She told Bob that she was the one who had had all the worries of bringing up the family, that *Bob* didn't have to worry, he had his job and his credit-card lunches and his trips all over the country and God knew what else. The Calloway home was highly charged; the smallest spark set off an explosion, and every explosion seemed to have the potential of escalating into the ultimate atomic blast that would blow the family apart.

So Bob Calloway "worked something out" with his son. Dick Calloway has agreed—for the time being—not to leave. He comes and goes as he pleases and gets as much money as he wants. He has his old room at home, but many nights he doesn't sleep there at all. He has been given a $6,000 sports car. He is not going to college; there is vague talk that he will enroll after taking a year off.

Is Dick Calloway happy? Not so that you would notice. In his contacts with his parents he is sullen and withdrawn. Are the Calloways happy? Emphatically not. Has leavetaking been forestalled? No. Dick has gone in all important respects. He remains at home only in a technical sense.

Audrey Del Grasso did and said all the right things when her son Robert turned out to be serious about a particular girl. "Bring Cheryl over to the house. We want to get to know her." Del Grasso spent time with Cheryl. They became good friends. When Robert announced that they were getting engaged, his mother was warm and loving and well-wishing and supportive in all the right proportions. After the wedding, when the couple moved to Columbus, Del Grasso was helpful about the practical aspects of the move and full of useful suggestions to her daughter-in-law about setting up housekeeping.

Robert and Cheryl came back east for Thanksgiving and

again for Christmas. They urged Robert's mother to come out and spend some time with them. Del Grasso said she would, but there was always some reason that the trip could not be made.

The letters diminished in frequency, particularly at Audrey's end. The young people were not able to come back to visit for Easter. One day Del Grasso was talking with a friend who commented on how well Robert and Cheryl were doing. "Oh," said Audrey Del Grasso, "I'm afraid you're wrong. There's trouble there. I can sense it. He's unhappy. I never said so much as a word against her, but I could see it from the beginning. It isn't going to work out. Nothing could do that little bitch but to get him as far away from here as possible. She knew damn well that I was wise to her. She's running around, you can bet on it. How much longer it can go on, I have no idea."

Ingrid Swanson is thirty-eight. She dresses as if she were eighteen—in faded and patched jeans, sandals, floppy blouses. She talks in what she considers the argot of youth. She spends time—a lot of time—with her children. She assumes the role of a peer, not a mother.

Her husband is bewildered, frustrated and embarrassed. So are her children. Ingrid's insistence on being a friend, not a mommy, increases their desire to spend time away from her. They think longingly of the future when they will be grown up and can move away. Every suggestion of the inevitable leavetaking spurs Ingrid into more excessive simulation of youth. She is trying to seduce her children into remaining with her.

The pain of the empty-nest syndrome is not diminished by the predictability of the event and the futility of resistance. Indeed, most parents who suffer from it feel worse, because at one level they are aware of the selfishness and folly of their feelings.

The best antidote for the syndrome is early and consistent

preparation of children for leavetaking. The parent who prepares his children is preparing himself as well. In subsequent chapters we shall examine the ways in which we may build strategies against the trauma of the empty nest.

# *V* WHEN OUR PARENTS GET OLD

THE FELLS and the Glazers had been friends for years. Earlier, when they got together their principal topic was the children. More recently the care and feeding of aging parents had gotten to be a primary focus of their conversation. There were so many ramifications: the limits of filial duty, the growing unreasonableness of the elders, the paucity of desirable options, the worry and strain, and, ever and anon, the financial aspects of the situation.

Finally it came down to three older people. Joanne Fell's mother was still alive, insisting stubbornly on living in the house she had lived in for forty years. Calvin Fell's father had moved into a small apartment in the city. Ned Glazer's mother, a few years younger than the other two, was still relatively active and spending most of her time in Fort Lauderdale.

The problem was becoming more acute for the Fells. Neither her mother nor his father could go on much longer on their own, it seemed. Money was not abundant in the family;

the parents did not have much, and while Calvin Fell was doing all right, he was fully extended financially in trying to keep up a suburban house and educate his three children.

Ned Glazer had gone up the ladder more rapidly. He was able to contribute toward the support of his mother, who had some money of her own. Nevertheless the Glazers were realistic enough to know that some tough decisions would not be long in coming.

The Fells clung to the notion that the institutionalization of their elders was the last resort. The idea of placing them in nursing homes was repellent. This attitude grew out of a gut conviction, which was strengthened by the evidence that facilities affordable on Medicaid and its derivatives were scandalously inadequate. Both of the Fells were scared by the thought of their parents being neglected in some heartless and inadequate Medicaid mill.

Ned and Rhoda Glazer took a more "modern" view of the situation. Their tendency was to urge that the old people be placed somewhere when they could no longer manage on their own. The reasoning went this way: "It's no favor to any-body to try to have them come and live with you. We've got our own lives to live. Aside from anything else, it's not fair to your kids. We're not doctors and nurses. The best thing all around is that they go into places that know how to care for them." The Glazers felt that their friends the Fells were ter-ribly old-fashioned in this respect.

But the Fells did bring their parents to live with them—first her mother, then his father. "It isn't as if we didn't have the room," said Joanne Fell. "The two younger kids are away at school most of the time, and Stan [their eldest] is off on his own. We'd be rattling around in the house. And besides, we have a responsibility . . . ."

As the Glazers and others had forecast, the situation in the Fell household was rough. The older people did not get along very well with each other or with anybody else. They were demanding. They wanted and sometimes needed more attention than their children were able to give them. True, the grandchildren appeared to get along all right with the senior members of the family, but the grandchildren were not carrying the burden. The Glazers shook their heads and determined that they would not make the same mistake.

Then Ned Glazer's mother seemed suddenly to lose a great deal of vitality and will. She was no longer capable of living by herself, in Florida or anywhere else. She expected that there would be a place for her with her son and his wife. "No way," said Ned Glazer. "She is going to be where she belongs and where she can be taken care of." He and Rhoda had been scouting extended-care facilities for some time. They had settled on a place: new, well-staffed, bright and clean. It was not hundreds of miles away, but it was not just around the corner either. The Glazers did not want a place too close. "Frankly, she would be expecting us to be dropping in all the time. That's bad for her and for us. We'll see her enough; and she'll have a chance to get acclimated to her new life."

The financial end of the proposition was not overlooked by Ned Glazer. He had long since decided on the proper course. He persuaded his mother to transfer her assets to him. "Let the government pay for her . . . that's what we pay taxes for." Ned Glazer's mother, whose protests were written off as crankiness, was installed in the facility.

The Glazers observed the increasing difficulties that the Fells were having in taking care of their parents. They were sympathetic. Their sympathy was not unmixed with the feeling that they had chosen the better way. They drove to see his mother whenever they could. In time the frequency of their visits declined. But they did keep in touch, as they saw it, and they said that the elder Mrs. Glazer was doing as well as you could expect. The facility was not quite the paradise they had anticipated, but it was not a hellhole either, and one had to face reality about these things.

The struggles of the Fells with their situation did not get easier, but the Fells appeared to make an accommodation with them. When his father got sick and went into the hospital, they were saddened and anxious, but resigned and not devastated. It became clear that Mr. Fell would not recover. He lasted two weeks in the hospital. His death was a melancholy moment, but a bearable one, made easier by the old man's own apparent reconciliation to the leaving of life.

Afterward the Fells felt closer to Joanne's mother. Not that she was any easier to get along with, but they were more inclined to put up with her. They had been through it all once; they were ready to go through it again.

The Glazers did not have these problems. Their problems were taken care of. Somehow, though, Ned Glazer was vaguely unhappy about it. He grew short-tempered. He would volunteer truculent defenses of what he had done with his mother, although nobody had asked him about it. Rhoda Glazer was silent and glum.

Then the news came that Mrs. Glazer had taken a very bad turn. She had fallen. She was in the hospital near the nursing home, critical. The Glazers went there immediately of course. They were there when she died. Now, six months after the funeral, the Glazers still tell each other, and their friends, that they did the right thing, and they adduce the evidence for this opinion, although no one questions their decision.

The problem of what to do with our elders is creating a society-wide culture for neurosis and, in some of its aspects, a gruesome scandal. It's getting worse. Study of fertility and mortality curves shows that the population, while still increasing, will be for a long time a population growing in old people and diminishing in young people. We keep our elders alive a lot longer than we used to; we are not bearing young at the rate we used to.

The burden of decision about the parents is falling on "children" who are no longer young but are, rather, well into middle age. We are faced with agonizing options about our parents at a time when we have many other worries and when we no longer possess the maximum emotional resiliency.

Developments of recent years have made it easy to warehouse the aged. Children are not legally responsible for their parents. Any responsibility that is undertaken is moral and voluntary. It is quite possible to denude the estates of parents and dump them on the government. Time was when this was simply not done. In a bygone age the assumption was that children cared for their parents till the end. Now the assumption is that children will do that only if they cannot afford anything better—or if they are old-fashioned. We send our parents away; to the Sun Belt if possible, while they are able to manage; to institutions when they cannot manage.

Our point is this: the placing of the aging relative is a common leavetaking situation today. The way in which it is resolved may have traumatic consequences for the children who do the disposing.

There is an old Jewish story about a home in which the grandmother was forced to sit at a table apart from the rest of the family and eat out of a wooden bowl. One day the mother of the family came upon her six-year-old daughter clumsily trying to fashion a piece of wood.

"What are you doing?"

"I am making a wooden bowl for you so that when you get old like Grandma you too can sit apart from all of us."

In our treatment of our own parents we are creating role models for our children. If your approach is to warehouse the old people somewhere out of sight, then this approach is transmitted to our own sons and daughters. An attitude of unfeeling relegation of the elderly is passed along as being the normal course of thought and action.

Without taking a rigid moral position, we point out that the warehousing of aging parents does not necessarily resolve the dissonances set up in the minds of the children who adopt this method of taking care of the problem. The elders are removed from sight, but not from mental and emotional awareness. A person may feel that he is being logical and "up to date" when he decides to place his mother in a nursing home. He will have all of the rational arguments at his fingertips. But he is still likely to be troubled—and he will not know why. He has convinced himself on the surface of his mind that he has done the right thing, but at a deeper level his feeling of responsibility remains. We see this over and over again today. The nagging sense of responsibility erodes emotional health. The death of the parent does not settle the matter. The survivors cannot escape the feeling that they did not do what they might have done—and should have done.

These considerations make it vital that we question the neo-wisdom that dictates institutionalization of the old when they lose strength. It may be that a coalescing of social currents will give new impetus to a movement to take aging parents into our homes. As mothers go out to work, the question of what to do with the children grows in importance. We are coming into a situation in which warehousing is becoming the norm at either end of the life spectrum. We warehouse the old because they are a nuisance; we warehouse the youngsters because to care for them would inconvenience us by keeping us from fulfilling ourselves.

Maybe we will come to see, more and more, that our parents can be brought to live with us earlier than is usual at present, and that they can fill an important role in taking care of our young children. Of course there are problems with this. Many mothers who have adopted this course complain that their children band with the elders against the parents: "Your son, my father, our enemy." In such situations there should be a prearranged psychological contract that the parents make the rules and have the ultimate authority, which may not be challenged by the grandparents. Obviously, conflicting messages from two sources of authority will leave a child thoroughly confused and ambivalent, leading to unfortunate consequences.

Whatever the ultimate resolution, anyone who is thinking about placing a parent in a "home"—rather than his own home—will do well to consider the price he may have to pay in leavetaking trauma.

# *VI* GETTING FIRED

THE SCENE is a suburban hardware store. The owner is selling a customer a pair of pliers. A teen-age boy stands behind the counter. As the owner rings up the sale he is talking to the boy: "Brian, I want you to understand that this has nothing to do with the quality of your work or how much we like you. It's just that we don't need the extra help any more." Brian looks defenseless, hurt.

A middle-aged man sits on the edge of a chair in a large office. The man behind the desk, slightly younger, is saying, "George, you've been around long enough to know how these things go. The problem is organizational chemistry. Nobody's at fault. I can't tell you how much I hate to do this, but I have to tell you that we have decided to make a change."

Brian is luckier than George by about thirty years. Getting fired is unpleasant when you're young. When you're older it can be a disaster.

For a lot of people—particularly men—the job has become

the paramount factor in life. Once it was a means—now it is an end in itself. The man who becomes involved in his job sends out tendrils of his being toward his occupation. He becomes entwined with it. Then he becomes part of it. He gives of himself to the job, and it nourishes him. The job grows to be everything meaningful in life, and (as we discuss elsewhere) it serves as an all-purpose excuse for neglecting those elements of life that he does not find meaningful any more. Is he preoccupied? Does he ignore his wife and children? Does he stay away from home? Drink too much? It's the job. As long as he is able to hold his job, he is a functioning human being; he need apologize for nothing.

So the husband's job becomes the San Andreas Fault of the marriage. While he is in it, there are groans and strains along the seam. When he loses it, it's an earthquake. A 1974 survey of psychologists and psychiatrists disclosed that clinicians consider getting fired to be one of the most traumatic and dangerous shocks that life can offer.

Why? To a considerable extent *guilt* is the cause.

The boss tells you you're through. You experience a welter of emotive reactions. You are angry. You are worried. You are shocked. And—this is true in so many cases—you are *shamed.* You feel guilty, even when there is nothing to feel guilty about. Somehow you are exposed before all the world as inadequate.

In another section of this book we consider the signals that should tell you it's time to take leave of your job. We speak of the slight tremors that tell you the occupational ground is shifting beneath your feet. But, as all experts in the field acknowledge, these are easy to ignore. We have such a stake in the job that the loss of it is unthinkable; thus we block out the possibility. The worker who is fired is often the only one in the place who is surprised.

Job termination is a severe form of leavetaking. When it happens to you, you face three vital tasks. The first is economic survival. The second is getting another job. These are tasks that reasonable people recognize and act on.

It is the third task that is so often ignored—at great cost. This is the need for *psychological survival*. You need a means of keeping yourself and your family together emotionally. You need a *psychic survival kit*.

For one thing, you need some "myth medicine." There are a lot of myths about getting fired.

*Myth:* Getting laid off is a blessing in disguise.

*Fact:* The notion that getting fired can be the making of a man is part of what H. L. Mencken called the American Credo —but it's not true. Getting fired is a severe setback. Understanding the severity of the situation may be one of the keys to keeping it from turning into a personal catastrophe.

*Myth:* When the boss lays you off, you should "take it like a gentleman."

*Fact:* There is no reason why you should make it easy for the boss. Be as tough as you can and get as much as you can in severance pay, time for job hunting, and use of the premises as a job-hunting base. You have no reason at all to feel guilty. And if the boss does feel guilty about it, well, that's *his* problem.

*Myth:* Right from the moment of firing, you should "keep a stiff upper lip."

*Fact:* You are hurt and angry. If you try to keep your emotions bottled up inside, they will turn back on you. You will begin to blame yourself. Richard Hunter of the National Association for Mental Health observes that a decline in real income is a problem most of us can handle, but if the individual sees the decline as the reflection of his own failure, he suffers a depression that can become acute. So for a few hours after you are fired, *do* express your emotions fully. Tell your boss how you feel. Tell your wife. Get it off your chest.

*Myth:* It's important to keep the news from children.

*Fact:* Even very little children are sensitive to atmosphere. They will know that something is seriously wrong. If a child is kept in the dark, he will worry more, feeling that he may be responsible. Tell the kids.

*Myth:* To talk about money makes things worse.

*Fact:* Pollster Daniel Yankelovich concluded after an extensive study that many Americans are not equipped to cope with economic difficulty "either psychologically or in terms of money management." The problem is made worse by the fact that "money is a taboo subject in many homes." It may not be pleasant to talk about money or the lack of it, but avoiding the issue will prove to be far worse.

*Myth:* When people love each other, adversity brings them closer.

*Fact:* This may be so for *some* couples, but adversity, if not handled well, can destroy the most seemingly solid marriage. Typically, the man moves from frustration to depression, withdraws into snappish remoteness, and, because of a combination of preoccupation and functional impotence, abandons all semblance of affection. At the same time, the woman offers support but is continually rejected. She then becomes angry and self-pitying, and finally comes to share her husband's feeling that he is inadequate.

You need "survival splints." Here are some techniques for support that can heal the break.

*Be absolutely realistic and open.* Take your most pessimistic estimate of how long you'll be out of work—and then double it. Do your darkest nightmares say six months? Figure a year.

*List all possibilities for income and decide to make full use of them.* Unemployment compensation? Of course! Food stamps? By all means. Some of the most affluent-looking people you see on the street may be using them. Get the information about food stamps and how to qualify for them from your local unemployment office.

From whom can you borrow money if necessary? There may have been a time when you'd rather die than ask Uncle Dan for a loan, but it's a new ball game. You may not want to make the touch now, but lay the groundwork.

Hold family meetings and lay it on the line. Getting a job may be easier for your wife than for you. If that's so, let her do it. And let the children help out wherever they can.

Tell your neighbors and friends. They may be of real help— in keeping their ears open and telling you about job possibilities. Remember, however, that the new position is most likely to be found through your own efforts. Don't count on search firms or other external forms of assistance. They often promise more than they can deliver. Also, they may make you feel too dependent.

*Keep up your relationship with the world.* When people invite you out, go! Since you are being candid about your situation, they won't expect you to reciprocate for the time being.

Find someone outside the family to talk with, to listen to you and perhaps counsel you during your most unhappy moments. A clergyman is trained to fill this role. You don't have to be regularly participating in religious services to talk with him, although you may find going to a church or synagogue a solacing and refreshing experience.

Find out if there is a group of unemployed people meeting occasionally at the local church, community center or union headquarters. There are more such groups being formed every day. If there is none in your neighborhood, you may want to think about organizing one. Talking to others who find themselves in the same circumstances will be helpful on many levels. Take some adult courses. High schools and Y's often have low-cost adult-education programs. A course can be another source of interest as well as a way to meet people and learn things that can be profitable and broadening.

*Find ways to live cheaply but not miserably.* Organize the household into a "taut ship." Turn off the lights, keep telephone logs and budget all expenditures. A lot of people, older or younger, have found there is heightened pleasure in orderly living, even when that order is imposed through necessity.

*Don't cut out entertainment, but revise your priorities.* Previously, on a scale of one to five, drinks, dinner and dancing might have rated "one," while a trip to the movies was a "three." Lop off the expensive items on the scale if they are near the top. Now the movies may rate as a "one," with a trip to the zoo or a museum as a "two."

*Explore new options for pleasure and, maybe, profit.* Are you good with your hands? Do you have a green thumb? You may be able to make some money by using skills you acquired during leisure activity.

*Keep up the amenities of courtesy and civility even when you don't feel much like it.* This is not hypocrisy; it is survival. Nobody is going to give another job to a sorehead with a chip on his shoulder.

*Use the lever of frugality to pry yourself into better physical shape.* Admit it, you probably feel better without those three-martini business lunches. Do some daily exercises. You can't use the excuse that you don't have the time. Walking and cutting out snacks can save money and make you feel better.

*Bad as things may seem, realize and act on the fact that your joblessness carries with it certain flexibilities in your schedule that you have previously not enjoyed.* Suddenly you have time to talk to your wife, children, and friends, to take a leisurely walk, enjoy a beautiful day. Try to make the most of your freedom whenever you can.

And you need "post-termination therapy." Effective therapy

is, almost by definition, healing that is practiced by one person on another. You cannot go it alone; you cannot heal yourself.

The wife of a man who has been fired from a job in which he was thoroughly involved has an important role to play. The therapeutic elements in her kit include *support, realism* and *tenderness.*

*Support.* He is down on himself, and he feels he has let you down. Sometimes he will seem to try to provoke you into recrimination. Don't be provoked. Concentrate on the good things he has done and the better things he will do.

*Realism.* At the same time, the wife of the fired man has to see things clearly. She cannot go along with—and add momentum to—his wild swings between optimism and pessimism. Balance must be her bag. Doctors and nurses do what will make the patient better, not what the patient wants. Psychoanalyst Robert Seidenberg observes that "countless women in this situation have, against their better judgment, supported harebrained schemes and business ventures of their newly unemployed spouses rather than appear uncooperative." Forced leavetaking from a job is not conducive to balance and clarity of vision. These the partner should be prepared to supply.

*Tenderness.* Support and realism are potent healers when they are administered in an atmosphere of affection. The wife of the man who has lost his job cannot make the experience fun, but she can encourage him to appreciate some of the positive side effects of his new—albeit unwanted—freedom. One wife said, "Our marriage was a sexual zero for ten years. During the day he was at work. At night it was 'Don't wake the kids.' On weekends he was too tired. When he got fired we had lots of worries, but after the first shock he was able to become a lover again."

When you become convinced that firing is inevitable, it's better to take the initiative and take leave of a job before it takes leave of you. One executive observes that the best antidote for termination is to "live in a perpetual state of resignation." You want to be a resource rather than a reject. This is not always possible; so have your psychic survival kit well stocked. The most seemingly secure of us may have the greatest need of it.

If you can handle the situation of being fired, it may be the mortar that keeps your marriage together forever. A rueful executive told us, "My wife blamed me for losing my job, and I never forgave her for not standing by me." The positive side of this coin is to build emotional capital in critical times.

### What Happens When You Quit?

Getting fired is a shock. The pangs of leavetaking come in a rush. Some of them are extremely painful. But you don't escape leavetaking problems by leaving a job voluntarily. The problems are different, but they come.

A woman quit a job she had held for twelve years. She talks about her feelings: "You weigh the pros and cons of leaving on the basis of hard facts. You think about money and opportunity. You don't think about the emotional hangups until they happen to you.

"You don't realize the extent to which you will miss what you're leaving until you've made the break. At that point you vacillate. You want to undo it all, make things go back to where they were. You ask yourself, 'Why am I leaving? Things really weren't so bad. How can I be sure they'll be better in the new job?,' etc., etc.

"You want the people you are leaving to feel sad and bereft because you're going away. You want them to think that you did your job so well that you can never be replaced. But on another level, you don't want to leave them in a hole; you'd like to feel that you managed things so well that they can keep going without missing a stroke. You want them to get along without you, but you don't want them to get along *that* well.

"And you tend to hang around too long, draining the situation, bleeding it dry, making emotional demands on the people you are leaving and on yourself.

"It is not until you start to think, I am wiser and richer for having spent so much time with you, and I will always have good memories of you, that you begin to come to terms with leaving.

"Going away reveals more about yourself than most situations do. This is one of the truest statements ever made. If you are going to be able to say goodbye to someone or something close to you, you have to take a long, hard look at yourself. I did. I didn't like everything I saw, but I felt better because I knew myself better."

You can prepare yourself to leave a job by thinking about and trying to evaluate a number of factors.

Before making the decision, consider the emotional element. Recognize the degree to which the job is not just a means of earning a living but a relationship that has become part of your life. The workplace is, to a considerable extent, your community.

This doesn't mean that you should remain in a job because you have emotional ties to it. These things change; you will form attachments on the new job. But by thinking about all of the things you're taking leave of, you will be better prepared to hande the strain of parting.

Anticipate ambivalence. Only after you have made the firm decision to leave will you realize fully the grip that the old job has on you—your ties to the people, your involvement in the routine. You'll want them to miss you; and at the same time you'll want them to manage without you.

Once your decision is made, stay around long enough to honor your obligations for adequate notice. But don't make it an emotional orgy. You'll have qualms. Keep them to a minimum by concentrating on work rather than on extended farewells. Save the tearful goodbyes for one concentrated burst during your last day on the job.

Focus on the good things: the experience you gained, the friends you made, the good will you leave behind. Understand that the leavetaking you have initiated is a sign of maturity and a necessary element of growth.

Finally, be fair to the organization you're leaving and to your successor by training him or her, so that the benefits of your experience and wisdom will not be lost. Don't leave the next person between the rock and the hard place.

# VII UPROOTS: THE MOVE TO A NEW COMMUNITY

THE CORPORATE NOMAD is a Typhoid Mary of leavetaking trauma. As he hopscotches around the world—three years in Kansas City, three years in Paris, three years in New York— he experiences no real pain. Oh, it may be inconvenient to move so often, but he doesn't have to take care of the details, and in a real sense he never takes leave of what is important to him. He is plugged into his career.

Meanwhile his wife and children are subjected to a series of shocks. Life is a recurring drama of emotional and social isolation. The instigator, the mobile executive, is immune to its effects. He tells his family that he is doing it all for them.

Business traditionally has called for the commitment of the "whole man." Nobody rises to the top without making a total personal commitment. Part of the demonstration of commitment is being willing to subject others to being up-rooted and displaced like pins on a map.

Things are tougher for the manager who is not immersed in career above all else. He must undergo the torture of frequent transfer because he feels he has no other choice.

A hard-driven and hard-driving data-processing executive, seeking a vice-presidency, moved to stepping-stone positions in three competitive companies within a two-year period. Each move meant relocating his family. "This nearly killed my wife and kids," he said, "not to mention my seventy-two-year-old mother. A few months ago, when I had to pull my boy out of high school, tears were shed as his friends waved goodbye at the airport. My family really suffered, and I almost changed my mind. But I didn't. The opportunity was too great."

Some figures will show the degree to which the corporate executive is a man in motion. (The use of the masculine form here is still most appropriate.) According to 1975 census figures there are about 4.5 million Americans in the category of salaried managers and administrators. Within twelve months about 25 percent of them move for one reason or another. An average of industry figures and estimates shows that 400,000 will voluntarily leave their jobs. Another 300,-000 will be fired. And 700,000 will be transferred to another city or country.

This spate of executive peregrination has certain consequences. For one thing, the burgeoning practice of shifting managers from location to location has been a great boon to the $2 billion moving and storage industry. Movers are set up to relocate management people in first-class fashion.

*Business Week* (October 28, 1972) cited a survey showing that 68 percent of American managers in the twenty-five–forty age bracket move at least once every three years, 23 percent move every two years, and 18 percent move annually. Long-haul transfer is a way of life at places like GE, ITT, Standard

Oil of New Jersey. At IBM it became popular to explain the initials as "I've Been Moved." A senior executive of an oil company says bluntly: "Moving is the life's blood of our business—it's as simple as that. . . . If a guy wants to get ahead, he expects mobility. Growth means movement."

For many years managers have bought the idea that success is to be found in movement from job to job rather than by staying with one company. A survey of corporate presidents conducted in 1974 shows that executives who change companies make it to the top faster than those who stay with one firm for a long time.

However, by 1970 industry was confronting a novel form of insubordination. Executives were refusing to accept transfer. Then came the recession. Vocal resistance to transfers subsided. The moving vans began to roll again, and they have been rolling ever since. Corporate leaders have resumed the happy pastime of shifting executives around like pieces on a game board. Indeed, there is a new manifestation of the lust for managerial mobility. In 1974 Weyerhaeuser and General Electric began an experimental program of swapping executives between companies for temporary periods. Other corporations were said at the time to be eyeing this experiment with considerable interest.

However, there are counterdevelopments. Serious managers listen to the academic community, at least that portion of it that studies organizational affairs. And a growing number of academicians are looking askance at transfer as a way of corporate life.

The anthropologist Lionel Tiger observes that "an important consequence of the corporate commitment to moving managers around is that their wives and children are deprived of the fundamental human requirement of social continuity and personal stability; that the managers are debarred from becoming effective members of the communities in which they find themselves; and that by forcing people to adapt to the company's scheme, rather than adapting the company to the people who work in it, American business is disenchanting the sons and daughters of its own executives themselves."* Harry Levinson of the Harvard School of Business questions whether "just rotating a man around provides the kind of experience he should have today."

Women are digging in their heels. Many corporate wives are simply refusing to be shipped here and there in the baggage cars of their husbands' career trains.

The comments of professors and the obstinacy of wives count for something. An even more persuasive factor being considered by corporate czars is money. The costs of moving executives have risen sharply. It takes more than $20,000 to effect the average transfer of a manager within the United States. International corporations are bringing American executives home from Europe and replacing them with nationals. It's simple economics. After World War II European countries—eager for U.S. investment and know-how—offered large tax advantages to Americans. The relatively high purchasing power of the dollar added to the attractiveness and economy of shifting Americans overseas. Now it's different. The dollar has declined. The foreign tax loopholes are being closed. The compensation bill for the U.S. manager abroad has climbed out of sight. Add to this the cost of annual leaves for him and his family and tuition for his children in special schools—all borne by the company—and the cost becomes prohibitive.

Furthermore, there is the question, "When a manager is transferred, is he just as effective in his new post as he was in the old one?" A new discipline called Human Resource Accounting undertakes to translate human behavior into dollar figures. The evidence shows that it takes executives considerable time to get "up to speed" when they are shifted

* Lionel Tiger, "Is This Trip Necessary?" *Fortune,* September 1974.

into new locations, and of course even more time when they change companies. The money that this costs in on-the-job training, delays, and bad decisions cannot be measured with CPA-type accuracy, but the costs are high.

The tendency to move executives around like pieces on a game board will diminish. This will not come about because of corporate altruism but because of economic self-interest and common sense. So to some degree the velocity of managerial movement, which contributes so much to the incidence of leavetaking trauma, will be abated.

However, it will still go on. There will always be corporate nomads. Perhaps the ultralogical solution would be to prescribe that such dedicated individuals should never marry. They could constitute an elite corps, like the Janissaries of old Turkey, who were recruited from the Caucasus when young, prohibited from taking wives, used during their effective lifetimes, and then replaced. Such a practice would not perceptibly reduce the stockpile of willing young executives. The sons and daughters of the highly paid wanderers turn their backs emphatically on the route chosen by their fathers.

Nevertheless, as long as high mobility remains, to any degree, as a factor in advancement, there will be wives and children desolated by the effects of career leavetaking.

## The Moving Experience for Women

For the man who relocates for career reasons the move usually means advancement and greater challenge. For his wife it has the effect of a demotion. Robert Seidenberg points out that "the hardship for the woman ... is found in losses that accrue to her in particular, losses not only of friends or neighbors with whom she has grown comfortable but also of status that has come from accomplishment in the community where she resides. The name that she has made for herself in the social and societal sphere is not in a professional role."*

Most of the physical tasks and decisions connected with the move are loaded onto the wife. At the same time she loses friends and status. As Seidenberg points out, her credentials are not transferable. She must start all over.

This loss of community status may have profound psychological effects. The woman who has moved as supercargo on her husband's career ship may engage in dysfunctional and obstructional behavior. She wonders about her identity. She worries about the children. She complains of loneliness. Worst of all, she assumes all the blame for her difficulties. Women who are caught in this snare tend not to blame their problems on the move. With no other explanation, they impute to themselves base motives. Typically, an unhappy wife says, "I know this new job means everything to him, and yet I seem to be trying to sabotage it. What's wrong with me?" Her guilt is likely to be reinforced by the attitude of her husband, who thinks that everything would be perfect if she would only snap out of it.

Deprived of relationship with a community, the uprooted wife tries to create the facsimile of community within her own home and family. The family is unable to meet her needs for an end to social isolation. Her increasing demands overload the family's resources. As Seidenberg says, "The nuclear family must serve as an emotional supermarket where all things are supposed to be found—and also devoured."†

Result: the husband's ego blossoms while the wife's is destroyed.

The basic problem in this situation is one of traditional attitude. The wife assumes that she must accept uprooting because it is important to her husband. (As women continue

* Robert Seidenberg, *Corporate Wives—Corporate Casualties?* (New York: American Management Association, 1973).
† *Ibid.*

to build careers in business, there will be increasing cases in which it is the wife who is asked to move and the husband who is faced with the role of supercargo. The consequences will be even more destructive.)

The fact is that when a husband announces to his wife that the family will have to pull up stakes because he has a job opportunity elsewhere, he is engaging in an act of desertion. Only the wife's acceptance of the traditional role has saved husbands from the legal and emotional consequences of the act. When industry recognizes the part it plays as a home wrecker, and when career-oriented people accept more of the responsibility for the agonies of transplantation, the situation will improve.

Meanwhile far more women and children than men will continue to be asked to undergo the enforced social isolation that is part and parcel of corporate nomadship. There are certain things that women in such a position—or those who may confront the problem—can do.

Overall, it is important that mother and children build their inner resources. Relocation means loneliness. People, adults or not, who habitually stave off loneliness by getting in touch with friends—in person or by phone—are vulnerable to extreme hardship when they move to a new community in which these amenities are not immediately available. They cannot depend on each other for company. Those in a family that may have to hit the trail should practice doing things on their own—reading, pursuing hobbies, working. When we stock our own reservoirs of resources we can call on them for considerable sustenance in time of need. When we try to dip into each other, the resources quickly run out.

Too often the wife, upon whom the burden of finding a new place to live has fallen, tends to choose her new home using criteria that have nothing to do with easing emotional isolation. For example, a relocated mother will give high priority to finding a house that is convenient to her husband's job. Thus the husband, who is already garnering practically all of the benefits of the move, gets still another, sometimes at the expense of his wife's deepening isolation and unhappiness.

The convenience of the new home should be secondary. Its physical characteristics also are not as important as the potential of the location for offering entry into a new community relationship. Of course the schools are important; but the wife who chooses only on the basis of convenience for her husband and good schools for the children is short-changing herself in a way that will hurt her and ultimately everyone else in the family.

Look at the neighbors. Are they within your age range? Do they have children around the same age as yours? Do they devote the amount of time and effort to keeping up appearances that you would feel comfortable with? (For example, when one is not an assiduous gardener, it is asking for trouble to move into a neighborhood of highly manicured lawns, where people will sneer at your crabgrass.)

What is the dominant religion—if there is one? Where is the place of worship of your choice, and how active are its social possibilities?

Are there social and community activities nearby that will be congenial? What are the opportunities for women, volunteer or paid? How about the political cast of the community? Are there likely to be people whose interests and opinions coincide with your own? (A tennis player will be even more unhappy when she finds herself surrounded by people who prefer golf.)

In sum, the selection of the home may be the one most important option for self-preservation open to the relocated woman. She should exercise it to the fullest extent without feeling selfish or guilty.

# VIII THE BREAKUP

THE EXTRAMARITAL RELATIONSHIP offers a kind of laboratory of leavetaking. It may weave together various threads of the parting process, not all of them by any means involved with parting from another person. Some affairs have more to do with the problem of saying goodbye to youth and vigor. Others are given impetus by the "split chic" fashion of today, which confers higher ranks on the adventurer than on the stayer-put.

Engagement in an amour does not invariably signal leave-taking from one's spouse—nor should it. Some affairs are the making of a marriage—or, at least, the preventative of its undoing. True, some extracurricular liaisons make the marital parting inevitable. But others lead to breakup not because leavetaking is implicit in the existence of the affair but because those involved act in a way that leads to separation and divorce, even if this is not what they really want. The adventuring spouse behaves as if the out-of-bounds relationship were permanent, knowing that it is not. The straying male wants his mistress to say "Leave your wife," knowing that in the end he will choose the wife. The trouble is that this behavior can induce all concerned to take positions that result in the end of the marriage, though nobody desires it. The husband *wants* his wife to know. The wife, forced to know and acknowledge that she knows, is pushed into a position from which she finds it difficult to retreat. The mistress, having conventionally demanded that the affair be placed on a permanent basis, discovers that the imminent reality of such an arrangement is far from her heart's desire, but it appears impossible to undo what has been done.

We may classify affairs under three general headings.

*The offer you can't refuse.* Occasionally party A may be so attracted to party B—and find that attraction so wholeheartedly reciprocated—that rejection seems the ultimate folly. This kind of opportunity opens up for some and not for others. John F. Kennedy was never without the option. When Moshe Dayan was asked about his sexual alliances, he responded by asking in turn, "What would *you* do if beautiful women were always begging you?"

This species of involvement offers the least implicit threat to resumption of normal marriage. It can be a momentary episode that, yes, causes pain, but does no permanent damage. The result is frequently the end of the marriage, but that does not have to be the case.

*Getting out of the rut.* Another sort of sexual adventure comes into being as a result of boredom. The individual's existence is humdrum. Life is dull. He isn't necessarily seeking adventure, but when a chance meeting puts it in his path he says "Why not?" So he tries to romance his way out of the rut. The effort brings transitory stimulation and change. When the affair ends, there is no intrinsic reason why the marriage cannot be maintained, unless the events surrounding the liaison have so complicated the situation that leavetaking becomes inevitable.

*I'll show YOU!* The most damaging affair is entered into out of vindictiveness and hostility. Pleasure is secondary; the primary purpose is to strike back at a mate. Anger at indifference or injury, whether it is justified or not, provides the motivating power and the fuel. This kind of extramarital activity contains the maximum in explosive leavetaking potential.

We are concerned here with affairs indulged in by relatively normal people within our particular culture. For example, the extreme behavior of the compulsive womanizer does not fall within our purview. This individual has special problems. We see these problems manifested in his reactions to the Rorschach blots. Typically, he sees all women as either witches or Playboy bunnies. His wife (and perhaps his mother) is a witch; all other women are bunnies. Also, we do not speak here of nymphomania, a complaint that has been pointed out as being more readily diagnosed by writers than by physicians or psychiatrists.

Our conduct of affairs and our reactions to them are, in good measure, influenced by the culture in which we live. In the United States we accept the Old Testament view of man as an animal who needs taming. In other countries— Latin America, for instance—a man is perceived as odd and probably homosexual if he does not have a lover or permanent mistress.

Traditionally it has been the man who makes the running in this area. That is changing. Our attitudes toward male and female roles are of course undergoing considerable reappraisal. There was an interesting occurrence recently at a hospital specializing in surgery on hermaphroditic babies— infants born with both male and female organs. In such cases the choice may lie with the surgeon. He can make the baby one or the other.

The staff was convened to consider the question: When all other factors are equal, which should the doctor choose to create, a boy or a girl? Psychiatrists over fifty said "Girl," basing their response on the premise that a woman is destined for fewer troubles as a result of her sexual equipment. Men suffer from the agonies of nonperformance as well as from physical ailments connected with their genital apparatus; they are lifelong prey to pride and prostate. These psychologists felt that the woman, after all, can fake the orgasm.

The young staff members, particularly the females, reacted heatedly. That is an outmoded proposition, they said; the woman doesn't need to fake anything any more.

The increasing tendency for women to demand equality in sexual adventure places an additional, societally induced burden on the male. How does a husband cope with his wife's infidelity? It has always been the expected thing for men to stray; the assumption is built into culture and religion. But when woman errs, it is instant divorce, the scarlet letter, shame and disgrace. That this makes no logical sense does not alleviate the problem. We are still a macho society; we have no female equivalent for "cuckold" in our language.

Until our attitudes are shaped by changing behavior patterns, the wife's affair will continue to be much more likely to lead to permanent leavetaking than the husband's adventure.

When an affair occurs, it should not be assumed that the end of the marriage is at hand. What is the primary motivating factor? Overwhelming opportunity? Boredom? Hostility? If it is one of the first two types, the liaison need not cause a breakup. Even when the amour is of the "I'll show YOU!" variety, the marital relationship can be rebuilt.

In practice the marriage is usually more thoroughly damaged and permanently affected than need be the case, not because the extracurricular liaison is in itself a dominant leavetaking factor but because attitudes and societal pressures make the break inevitable. A husband or wife gets into an entanglement. There are agonies, tears, showdowns. All parties to it are forced into positions from which they cannot retreat. The result is the end.

Even when a marriage endures after the end of an affair, it is often not really resumed. Leavetaking has occurred, but the man and woman remain frozen in a legal yoke. They go through the motions, but there is nothing there.

It doesn't have to be that way. True, the affair almost always means leavetaking of a sort. But it may involve only parting with illusions of idyllic and monogamous bliss, illusions that were bound to be dispelled in any case, and that, truth to tell, aren't helpful to a mature and enduring relationship.

Let's dissect a very typical variety of affair, the one that grows primarily out of boredom with the familiar and a sense of time passing. As we look at it, we may see how different threads of leavetaking are woven through it, and how we often settle for an unsatisfactory resolution when it is not necessary to do so.

"She was the love of my life," he said, twiddling his third martini and studying the nonexistent tea leaves at the bottom of the glass, "but now it's all over."

Vincent Albrecht is forty-eight. He used to look younger—not any longer. He has been married for twenty-six years. The youngest of his three children is nineteen. For seven years Albrecht has been involved in an affair with Alice Lynn, now thirty-one, who used to be a research assistant in his department. Lynn quit and went to another company eight months ago. Albrecht has just learned that she will be married in three weeks.

"I let myself turn into a cabbage while he lived the high life of his goddamned expense account," says Denise Albrecht, forty-seven. "The worst was the humiliation. Did he think I didn't know what was going on? Maybe he's through with her now, maybe not—I don't know. I don't care. What's left for me now?"

"I went into it with my eyes open, I guess," says Alice Lynn. "But you always hope. You think it's going to last forever. Then one day you look around and you wonder what happened to the years. You wonder what's going to happen for the rest of your life. And the awful thing is you don't give a damn."

In this version the man has reached the mid-thirties at least. He has achieved enough success at work so that there is some discretionary money available to him. The conduct of an intrigue costs money. Nobody thinks of the financial aspects as paramount, but it is a necessary adjunct. The classic male adulterer spends money in the pursuit of his passion. At the same time he attempts to assuage his guilt by bringing home a decent salary to take care of the wife and family.

The man is restless. He finds himself tethered to a life whose outlines he can clearly see for the rest of his downhill years; and he deems the view unsatisfactory. "There must be something better, something else," he tells himself. He does not consider that he is a faithless person. He loved his wife and his kids, loves them still. But now he falls in love with someone else. The conventional wisdom is that you can't love two people at once, but this does not seem to apply in his case. He feels that somehow he is an exception.

The affair is not invariably work-connected. Sometimes the other party is a neighbor or an acquaintance or the wife of an acquaintance. Some years ago a New York writer went to Hollywood to work on a picture being produced by Otto Preminger. A few days after his arrival Preminger issued an invitation to a party: "Saturday night, my place; there will be a great many interesting people there." The writer, whose family was still back east, demurred: "I don't know anybody here, and I'd feel out of place. If you don't mind, Otto, I'll take a rain check." A couple of days later the writer received a phone call; an old classmate of his wife's was in Hollywood. On an impulse he asked her if she would like to go to a party at Otto Preminger's house. Eagerly she assented. When the writer next saw his producer he said, "Uh, about that invitation . . ." Preminger smiled. "Is it too late to change my mind?" the writer went on. "You see, there's someone in town . . . she's my wife's best friend . . ." Preminger's sardonic smile broadened. "It is *always*," he observed with Viennese urbanity, "the wife's best friend."

But it is not always the wife's best friend. Native caution and simple logistics are limiting factors. But there is a more encompassing reason why the affair so often involves a woman who is part of the working scene. The job constitutes a more stimulating milieu than the home and its surrounding community. It is on the job that this kind of man truly lives. Here is where the challenges lie; here is where he has most of his mental and emotional apparatus switched on. Around home his engine is usually on "idle."

He meets a woman at work. He sees her when both are at their best and brightest. She is usually younger. She has some brains and talent. Most of all she has energy. He and she talk about things that are of major interest to both. They solve problems together. She is a trusty companion on the professional hunting ground. In addition, she is an attractive female. Willy-nilly, he makes the comparison, without realizing what he is doing. There, back at the ranch house, is his wife—a lovely person, it is true, a loyal helpmate and a dedicated mother. But she is not interesting. The wife seems to have no existence in the dimension in which the man's existence is most vibrant.

Their intellectual life has cooled; so has their sex life.

There are no more adventures at home; at work, every day is an adventure, and the man becomes more and more enamored of his fellow adventurer.

The man is in a leavetaking posture. His marriage has turned into a relationship that does not challenge him and impinges less and less on his consciousness. It is comfortable; but we don't always put the highest priority on familiar comforts. Furthermore, he and his wife do not talk with each other about the things that are important to him. "My wife doesn't understand me" is another of those truisms that have achieved that status because they are true. Naturally she doesn't understand him; there is no chance for understanding.

He is ready to take leave of his previous state of life. Not completely, of course; he wants (without really acknowledging that he wants it) to move on into a new phase while preserving the umbilical cord to the old. The affair becomes, after a while, the inevitable choice.

Opportunities abound—trips, late meetings, professional propinquity. At some point the offer is made, subtly, by either party. The gambit may not be taken up at first. Finally, however, something happens. The incipient affair blossoms in bed.

Next day there are the agonies. "I must have been crazy. How can I do this to Denise and the kids? . . . There's no future for this at all. . . . The girl won't even speak to me today. . . . Maybe there's some way that we can just blot it out and go on the way we were before. . . . I will be blowing my career and my whole life if I let myself get involved."

He lets himself Get Involved. Passion comes out with a rush. He *knows* that this is really it; he was never in love before. For the first time he is really living. It's going to be worth all the anxiety and strain—and he knows there will be anxiety and strain. But there's no reason why Denise should ever find out about it. He will still fulfill his responsibilities;

he will be a good husband and father. After all, these things happen. There's nothing that anyone can do about them.

He may think, to some extent, about a full leavetaking—cutting loose completely through separation and divorce. But there are his obligations; there are the children. His partner may not desire marriage at this stage. He has second thoughts about it.

So he goes on, knowing that the situation cannot endure forever, but acting as if it can. He is hooked into several leavetaking dilemmas. He wants to say goodbye to the family element of his past life in which he feels trapped, but he does not want to cut himself off completely from it. He is in the process of taking leave of the days of his youth and vigor; the current involvement is the major manifestation of that. His affair will not remain static. At some point there will be a culmination, which will entail final leavetaking of his wife, his mistress, or both.

One serious leavetaking problem is enough for anyone to try to handle at a given time, often more than enough. The man who is carrying on a liaison is locked into at least three. Add to this the possibility that his status and effectiveness at work may well be compromised by his amorous activities, and you put a fourth potentially traumatic leavetaking—parting from the job—into the mix. The strains are enormous.

The mistress is in a different position, but not a better one. She is likely to sense, more sharply than her lover, that the relationship will come to a close and that that event will not be good for her. Her situation is pretty close to being "no-win." She is likely to be abandoned. There is a lesser possibility—that the man will make the decision to leave his wife and stay with her. Even that chance offers a blessing that is by no means unmixed. One woman said, "I'd prefer he not give up his kingdom—just that he include me in."

Let's say Vince makes the agonizing decision to stay with Alice. More often than not, the man who does this wants to go all the way, through divorce, into a new marriage. In a sense Alice has wanted to get married to her lover, but as the possibilities of this increase, she may find her enthusiasm lessening. Does she want to spend the rest of her life with him? What happens to her career? Is it not logical to assume that they will break up after a few years? Then what?

The levers of decision in the leavetaking situation are, on the whole, out of reach of the mistress. She cannot make the man's decision for him. Her only options come down to continuing the relationship or breaking it off. Meanwhile she lives with the guilty knowledge—difficult to avoid altogether for even the most sophisticated person—of being what used to be called a home wrecker. (A woman who was having an affair with a married man dreamed that she saw two doors to the ladies' room in a hotel. One was labeled "Good Girls," the other "Bad Girls." She tried to go through the "Good Girls" entrance, but a sinister figure blocked her way, directing her to the other door.) And she has to wonder what a complete cutoff from wife and family would do to the man with whom, at the moment, she feels she is in love.

The options are even less positive for the wife. While there is no objectively logical reason why this should be true, the responsibility for the children devolves upon her. Her principal activity in the early stages of the affair is going on as if nothing were happening. Does she know about it? Yes, in a sense she always knows about it, with one part of her mind and one configuration of her emotions. She is aware of the changes in her husband's behavior: the unexplained, or feebly explained, late nights and overnight absences; the odd reactions toward her from his working colleagues when she happens to meet them; his long silences and periods of touchiness, interspersed with spasms of "family man" togetherness, which ring so falsely.

The wife is not really the last to know; she is, however, usually the last to acknowledge. Then comes the catastrophic moment at which, through some fluke—a letter left around the house, a phone call, a chance meeting in the city—the situation is revealed in a way that she can no longer ignore. She responds with rage: "I have thrown my life away to keep house for you and raise your children, and this is the thanks I get." She is humiliated: "I lose my looks and my shape and my brains while I am being a good little wife, and you hop into bed with some floozie." She loathes him: "I never want to see you again. Go to your whore!"

But she does not break it off. There are the children, there is the home, there is the whole life she has built. The fear of leavetaking almost always takes precedence over the impulse to cut short the detestable relationship. And this fear of leavetaking gives rise to the quixotic idea that, somehow, virtue will triumph and she will win.

The first thing that should be pointed out about this classic network of leavetaking involvements is that nobody "wins." In the act of "winning" one automatically becomes a loser. The best that can be hoped for is a resolution that gives all parties optimum chances to move on to the next phase of life, damaged as little as possible by the episode.

For everyone involved it is important to separate the "musts" from the "cans," the "already happened" from the "might happen," the reversible from the irreversible.

In a full-scale extramarital affair partial leavetaking has already taken place. The man has taken leave in one aspect of his role as a monogamous, family-oriented individual. He has left his youth behind him.

For the mistress the end of the affair is built into its beginning. The leavetaking often is destined.

The wife will never be the same again. She has been wrenched away from her status as a dweller in an idyllic world peopled by a faithful, breadwinning husband and happy, high-achieving children. And of course the children have become enmeshed in a leavetaking as well. Even the youngest—although they may not grasp all the nuances and details—know that something is wrong, that something bad has happened.

The man will do well to carefully consider the realities before their consequences are forced on him. Here are some of the paramount realities for his consideration:

He cannot continue to straddle; except in rare situations he will not maintain equilibrium.

His wife knows—whether or not she has admitted it to herself.

He must make a choice: break with wife and family; break with his mistress; break with both; or try to rebuild the marriage.

By waiting and continuing to try to straddle, the choice will be forced on him, and it is apt to be the most traumatic and destructive of all the possible options.

The present involvement has probably made him less aware of other ties—with his children, his friends, his community, his job. All of these associations are being affected now, and will be affected far more by the ultimate resolution. Whatever happens, he will carry a load of guilt. A resolution that does extreme damage to wife, family and mistress assures that he will be saddled with the maximum load of guilt.

He must go on to something new—a rebuilt set of relationships that meets present needs and conserves the positive elements of the past.

These are some of the considerations that should be faced by the man involved in the traditional affair. There are others. The important thing is that he face them and begin to apply to his personal life some of the abilities that have given him whatever success he's had in business.

The "other woman" has her own set of facts to face.

In the end, the man is likely to leave her.

Her passion for her lover is probably cooling, may have cooled considerably already.

A tenacious fight to "win" the man is not apt to result in anything approaching a satisfactory victory. Even if she gets him, she is likely to be getting an emotional basket case.

As time goes on, her situation deteriorates. She is permitting her social skills to atrophy and her chances of forming other relationships to drift past.

She is an unusual person indeed if she is able to live without assuming an increasing portion of the guilt that is rife in the situation. Sophistication and a "now" outlook are insufficient safeguards. She may be able to convince herself, with good reason, that the wife is a bitch, but what about the children?

For the wife there is a special set of leavetaking considerations. Chances are she can "keep" her husband. Two questions: Does she really want to? And on what basis?

She and her husband have definitely taken leave of a phase of life. The parting occurred some time in the past; the affair symbolizes it and compels recognition of the fact.

She can force a showdown, a full-scale confrontation. This will no doubt be a catharsis for her, but to what extent does she want to polarize the situation?

What resources does she have independent of wifehood/motherhood? If that is the only dimension in which she exists, it is insufficient. She has a responsibility to herself to develop her independent personhood. This does not mean, necessarily, taking off. It does mean formation of relationships that offer new and different satisfactions.

It would require an offspring of Pangloss and Pollyanna to say that this is a good situation. It is a melancholy, painful episode. But there are some useful lessons that can be learned by all parties.

When a full-blown affair surfaces, it may signal a distinct break with the past, especially if the affair is of the "I'll show YOU!" variety. If the affair falls within the first two of our three categories, it may not be traumatic. In most cases this is a break that should have been recognized and acted upon earlier. The important thing now is to complete the necessary leavetakings that have been started and to rebuild the relationships that should be rebuilt.

The participants in the triangle cannot count on the present state of their relationships to sustain them. All need to stride into the future as unencumbered as possible.

The question is not, as they used to say, "Can this marriage be saved?" It is, rather, *"Should* it be saved?" Love, in the form of single-minded absorption with another person, is gone. What's left? Is there, for example, the possibility of comfortable companionship between husband and wife? They are probably not real companions now, have not been for some time—which is one of the reasons that the affair got started. But can they become friends? Both husband and wife must now ask, "Do I really like her/him? If there are children, the pressure to maintain the facade of the marriage is great. Accept, for the moment, that this must be done. If all that either party can envision is a facade, with two people living behind it as strangers to each other, then there is serious reason to contemplate junking the marriage. The façade alone will not save the children. If kids are the only reason for staying together, then there is no reason. Parents yoked in animosity and sullen resentment do not raise well-adjusted children.

The soprano Martina Arroyo (quoted in *Opera News,* December 18, 1976) talks of her separation: "So parting became a thing to do for the sake of . . . not beginning to lie to each other . . . while there is pain, there's also the security of knowing someone really cares. If I needed him tomorrow he would come, and he knows perfectly well it's the same with me."

In the turmoil of breaking events, neither husband nor wife—particularly the wife—really knows whether retaining the marriage bond is the right thing to do. They have shifting inclinations about it, but they don't know. The only way to find out is by considering the alternatives. This is a matter of examining all of the debits and credits on the current balance sheet of the relationship, spotting trends, projecting those trends into the future. The view of the future must be compared, in reasonable objectivity, with the alternatives. And one cannot consider the alternatives until one has begun a realistic assessment of needs and of the kinds of possible new relationships that will assure satisfaction and growth.

First priority must be given to examining the possibility of continuing the marriage—not reestablishing the past or maintaining a façade for the sake of the children or the neighbors, but rebuilding the relationship into something viable that meets the needs of both parties. The wife, who has not had a leading role in the creation of the situation that has led to the crisis, now assumes a paramount position. What she decides and how she handles things are vital. By her actions she may harden the position and close out the option of a renewed marriage or she may lay the groundwork for an association that will be different but perhaps better.

Here are some points that she should consider.

Is this his first affair or is it part of a pattern?

What message is he sending? Is it one of boredom, or of lost youth, or one of anger?

She is angry, and probably with good reason. There is no reason for her to feel guilty about her rage. The question is, should she permit her anger to provoke confrontations that will lead to an emotion-drenched breakup in which nobody has considered the long-range effects?

Can she overcome obsession? Some wives, fully aware of what is going on, immerse themselves in a search for needless corroborating detail—looking for letters, listening in on phone calls, spying. This is not constructive; it can trigger off the unwanted confrontation.

What are the possibilities for communication? Granted, communication is difficult. However, in a moment of calm she should tell her husband how much she has been hurt and that she would like to explore the chances of resuming the marriage. We heard of a wife who confronted her husband about his mistress. He said, "Okay. It's true. But do you want to give up twenty-five years of marriage and a secure home and position over this issue?" The wife relented. The next day at a pool club she saw her husband's best friend with a strange woman. She asked her husband about this. He answered, "I'm sorry to tell you that that is John's mistress." The wife went over, looked the young lady up and down, and then returned to her husband to say, "Ours is better looking."

Does this husband realize what he will be losing? Affection and understanding are much more apt to influence him than constant reminders of the affair. He should be given a chance to talk and consider.

Can she avoid "going public"? She needs a confidant, but pouring her heart out to a friend or relative may have an effect opposite to what is intended. The more public the affair, the more social pressure to save face. Many marriages that might otherwise be reconstituted go down the drain because of considerations of what "they" will think. Once this was a factor that facilitated reconciliation. In these days of split chic it is a divisive element.

In short, the strategy for the wife who wants to keep alive the marriage option is to ventilate her feelings without extreme passion and keep communications open without provoking confrontation. If objective consideration demonstrates that there is nothing in the marriage, then it may be time to end it. But it is vital to consider what will replace it.

Unhappily, marriage partners often come to different conclusions. Traditionally, in such a situation the husband wanted his "freedom"; the wife wanted the relationship to continue. Nowadays the woman is much more likely than before to be the one who wants the break. If one mate is adamant about parting, then this has to become a paramount consideration for the other mate, no matter how many reasons the latter may be able to adduce for going on. If A is determined that it's over, then it's over, no matter how tenaciously B may be able to fight a rearguard action. Some marriages go on for twenty years after one party has called it quits. This is not an outcome that benefits anybody.

The mistress should, as a matter of common sense, crank the end of the affair into her deliberations from early in the game. This is an episode, no matter how deeply it may involve her. It is a point on a curve, and the direction is downward. She should examine the association to determine the ways in which it has given her what she needs and the ways in which it has fallen short. Perhaps the sexual exploration has been thrilling, but the enforced absences of her lover have awakened in her an awareness of the importance of companionship and mutual support. Her next network of associations need not involve marriage, but she should look for the satisfactions that she did not get from the past liaison. In fact the affair may have been therapeutic for her by giving her a model of the kind of person she would like to seek in the future. Many women become "unfrozen" in an affair; thus they are enabled to go on to a more lasting relationship.

Overall, the conventional affair can be seen to have some usefulness as an enforced leavetaking, or, rather, syndrome of leavetakings that have already happened but that have not been acknowledged. As in some other kinds of leavetaking, the events, however painful, contain at least the seeds of growth. Both parties are compelled to recognize the goodbyes they have said—to illusions, to habits, to routines, to comfortable assumptions, to a stage of life that is now past.

For the affair is not the future. It is the past manifesting itself in the present. Obviously there are exceptions; some extramarital associations sustain themselves with mutual benefit, even to the discarded party. But much more often than not this continuation is as much of a façade as the forcibly retained marriage relationship.

The best possible outcome of a liaison is that, after the shock wears off, all concerned examine their present and future needs, discontinue the associations that no longer mean anything, rebuild those that should be rebuilt, and form new relationships they need.

In that way the end of the affair is a beginning.

### The Other Side of the Coin

It is implicit in our cultural history that women have borne more of the pain of leavetaking than men. That's changing. Here is one example.

The Maltzers were a typical suburban family. Allan commuted to a good job. Ruth tended to their two beautiful children and did good works in the community. The Maltzer children achieved good grades and moved on a steady course toward Ivy League universities. The friends of the Maltzers enjoyed them, valued them and envied them at the same time.

The marriage broke up. Ruth Maltzer remains in the house. The place is going to hell; Ruth no longer slaves in the garden, seizing avidly upon each tiny weed. She goes to consciousness-raising sessions. Her drive and powers of persuasion, once put to use under the banner of the PTA, are employed to enlist other women in the liberation movement. The children are pretty much on their own, they drift around town, but they seem happy. Ruth has taken a female lover.

Allan has an apartment in the city. He returns to the suburban town often. He tries to see the kids when they are available. He does things around the house; last month he painted the porch, which badly needed it. When he and Ruth see each other they speak cordially but remotely. Allan does his best to be friendly with Ruth's new companion.

As far as his own companionship situation goes, it scarcely exists. Just after the breakup of a marriage that had been under excruciating strain for three years, he felt free, exhilarated. On his own in the city, he looked up old friends, men and women. He was introduced by a divorced workmate to the singles-bar scene, met some girls, went to bed with a couple of them. Lately he hasn't been doing that. He hasn't been socializing at all. There is no real hope of getting back together with Ruth; Allan knows that. He doesn't know what to do. He is miserable.

Once upon a time when a marriage broke up, the wife was invariably considered the victim. She was left with the children. She would have to make her way in an alien world, in which she had lived only through her husband and the children. As for the man, he was now free, a bachelor again, able to enjoy all the formerly forbidden pleasures of being on the town.

This image persists, though it has a lot less basis in fact than it used to have. Marital leavetaking is exacting a greater toll from a lot of men than it is from the women with whom they have broken. To an increasing extent it is the newly freed woman who is able to arrange alternate associations with drive and purpose. She does not have to go as far as Ruth Maltzer. She can find a niche in life that gives her *status* and *function,* those attributes that the sociologist Max Weber deemed to be so important to modern life. She has the status of a liberated woman, and with it she enjoys the feelings of being recognized (by her peers) as one who has escaped domination. Her function is to create a new life for herself, proving in the process that she is as good as any man.

All of this is an inevitable and no doubt healthy reaction against the imbalances of the past. But it has the collateral effect of making leavetaking very difficult for many men. The man is still seen, in general, as the villain of the melodrama. He takes leave, not just of his wife but of his children and his home. His options for alternate relationships lack the fresh attractiveness of those available to the "now" woman. He can immerse himself in work, but he has probably been doing that already to a considerable extent. He can try to find a substitute wife through such established networks as Parents Without Partners or via the singles-bar route. After the first blush of novelty and the thrill of anticipation wear off, these courses may become arid and humiliating.

Meanwhile he worries about the children—probably more than he worried about them when he was around. He thinks their mother is not doing the right things concerning them, but he hasn't much recourse. The children may be friendly toward him, but they stop thinking of him as a father. He is an occasional playmate, a Santa Claus who arrives every other weekend. His authority and position are diminished. Or the kids turn against him. That's worse.

Perhaps his wife takes a lover, or a series of lovers. (Bad enough when they are male; if they are women his anguish is multiplied.) He may acknowledge intellectually that he has done the same kind of thing, or tried to do it, and that his former wife has just as much right to sex as he does. But emotionally it is extremely hard for him to handle.

He fears another marriage. He is exhausted by the rigors of the previous one and he feels that he could not go through another bad one.

He may try to maintain his old circle of friends, but this becomes more and more difficult. The very logistics are a problem; he is the one who has moved away. And now he is "different"; he does not fit into the circle any more. (Of course this is apt to be just as true of his ex-wife. But she is also likely to enjoy more sympathy if she wishes to continue to see her old friends, particularly female ones. And there is a more lively set of alternatives open to her.)

Overall, the man's status and functions have been severely eroded. A changing society has conferred the possibility of an existence with more purpose on the woman who has taken leave. This does not necessarily make leavetaking any easier for women, but it has made it a lot harder for men.

We write of the breakup, not the divorce. Divorce is a post-leavetaking process. Its procedures are painful; they are extensions of the anguish of the parting that has already taken place. The details of divorce can be tedious. Nevertheless they may serve a useful purpose. They are things that one must do, somewhat analogous to the rituals that follow death.

There is rage, guilt, the allocation of blame. There is the problem of what to do about the children. Such concomitants of this particular traumatic leavetaking are discussed later in the book when we take up the matters of preparation for leavetaking and strategies for carrying it out in the least damaging and most positive manner.

# IX RETIREMENT: PARTING FROM YOUTH AND POWER

GETTING OLDER is particularly hard on those whose life and livelihood are predicated on youth.

"I can play. I definitely can play third base as good as anyone. I can't hit a home run like I used to, but there's no reason I can't hit my lifetime batting average if I play every day. I'm concerned about playing two more years. I feel I can. I'm being realistic. I can play, I can do a good job."

The speaker is Brooks Robinson. Robinson is a third baseman for the Baltimore Orioles, one of the great all-time third basemen. He will be in the Baseball Hall of Fame.

Why is Robinson saying these things? It is August 1976. During the previous season Robinson batted .201, thoroughly inadequate for a major leaguer. Now he is hitting .200. Robinson is thirty-nine years old. He is on the bench. Third base for the Orioles is covered by a player fifteen years younger, a man who will never come close to Brooks Robinson at his peak.

Robinson says, "I love to play. I'm not in a hurry to hang it up. I'm not saying I'm going to play forever, but playing is more fun than anything else I can think of."

Jim Palmer of Baltimore is thirty. He is at the peak of his career, one of the best pitchers in the game. He says, "When you stop playing, it's not just one phase of your life that's over. Really, for most ballplayers their life *is* over, what you devoted your whole life to. Finished."

It's not just ballplayers. None of us finds it easy to face the realization that we grow old, that the time comes when we cannot do what we were once able to do. So we fight the advancing years.

For many the fight focuses on the concept of "retirement." Economic considerations and longevity curves have pushed retirement age downward, but at the same time there is a growing feeling that it is foolish and inhuman to turn people out to pasture when they have reached an arbitrarily chosen age.

Retirement—with all of the dismal connotations it carries for many individuals—means more than a symbol of aging. It is significant leavetaking from vigor and *power*.

Amid all the paraphernalia of office bestowed on John F. Kennedy when he moved into the White House, it is said that the single thing that fascinated him most was that he could push a button under his desk and then look out the window to watch a helicopter land on the lawn.

The obverse side of this coin is the distress suffered by Presidents when they leave power. It feels, said William Howard Taft, "like a giant locomotive pulling a toy train." The rest of the ex-President's life looks all downhill. Men who have sat at the pinnacle of power, when separated from that power get the equivalent of the "bends" felt by divers who come to the surface too fast.

Congress has voted to give ex-Presidents certain vestiges of power—office space, personnel, protection. The ostensible purpose of these privileges is to assist the former leader in handling the business matters—correspondence and the like —that are assumed to remain with him, and to safeguard his person. The real benefit of the law seems to be that it acts as a decompression chamber in which the ex-President can make some kind of adjustment to ordinary life.

The pangs of separation from power are not, of course, confined to Presidents. They beset most public servants who leave office; and they afflict individuals in the private sector who depart from jobs in which they cut a great swathe. The effect is most spectacular in the cases of those who have been high in government. A onetime world figure who leaves government need not be strapped for money; indeed he may be able to make a lot more money than he did on the public payroll. But he no longer has the staff, the Secret Service, the airplane on call, the band playing "Hail to the Chief," the fanfares, the protocol, and the platoons of reporters lusting to tell an eager world about his every move.

Saying goodbye to power is a severe leavetaking. Few escape at least some measure of its pain. Most of us, naturally, would be quite willing to risk future trauma for a taste of sweeping potency, but that doesn't make it easier to leave it.

There are ways in which we can inoculate ourselves against the hurt of leavetaking from power. The basis of the vaccine is self-knowledge, which enables us to clarify the situation and recognize the habit-forming elements of the dominant position.

We begin by making the distinction between power itself and the trappings of power. Kennedy's power entailed the awesome capacity to send the troops ashore at the Bay of Pigs, blockade Cuba, push the button that would release the missiles, freeze wages and prices, change millions of lives with a stroke of the pen. The helicopter that lands on the lawn is part of the *trappings* of power—the icing on the cake or, more accurately, the sugarcoating on the pill. The possession of great power is not in itself exhilarating for most people. It is a burden. The burden is made far easier to bear by the paraphernalia that accompanies power.

The ability to wield power can become a surrogate for brute force and supersex. People were shocked when the Nixon White House transcripts were released. They were appalled by the vulgarity and callousness of the talk in the Oval Office. But this is the way people of vast influence talk. "She's going to find her tits in the wringer. . . . We'll let him twist slowly, slowly in the wind. . . . I am going to stick it to those sons of bitches. . . . Screw him before he screws you. . . ." The chief executive officer of one of the world's largest corporations (an organization with a staid and sedate image) was well known for a favorite expression. Whenever a subordinate manager had done a thing to displease him he would exclaim, "I'll cut his balls off!"

The recurring references to violence and sex in the ordinary conversations of powerful people—when they are talking about matters on which they may bring their power to bear—are no accident. Power exerts a very personal influence on those who hold it, and the influence is manifested in atavistic and sexual terms.

The Watergate conspirators were all males. When we consider the plight of politicians who must leave office, we are, in the nature of things, talking about men. But the seductions of power are not confined to one sex. The woman mayor of a small city, defeated for reelection, says, "In an awful lot of ways it was a headache. Did you ever have breakfast with the head of a Teamsters' local? The interest groups, the complainers, the angle-players—none of them are ever satisfied, and they are a constant pain in the ass. There is almost never enough money to do what should be done, and on the rare occasions when you do get something good through, there is always a battery of lawyers to tie it up in court. But, oh, the chauffered car! The policeman saluting you on the steps! The phone in the back seat of the limousine! The trips to mayors' conventions! It is all so damned hard to say goodbye to!"

You get the promotion you have dreamed about. Now you are at, or near, the top of the heap. It is a smaller heap than that surmounted by the President of the United States, but it is your heap. Now you are—within your sphere—mighty. Your decisions will set important things in motion. You hold people's futures in the palm of your hand. You can hire and fire. You are an influencer of events.

For all this you receive money. The money is good, and welcome. It enables you to buy things you could not buy before.

But the real kicks may well come not through the exertion of mightiness or the spending of money but through the accompanying trappings of your newly acquired power. You have status, you have prestige. It is not just that you are important; people *know* you're important, and you are accorded certain manifestations of that importance.

These things are peripheral. They are the toys of the mighty. Yet they are habit-forming. When you are cut off from this position, what you will probably miss most is not the onerous responsibility of making big decisions and the constant demands on your time and attention, or even the money you are paid, but rather the adjuncts of dominance—the symbols of your position.

Few of us can withstand the seduction of the paraphernalia of potency. They grow on us. Leaving them can be a terrible wrench. It can be worse than that. Separation from power can destroy a person.

The best way to inoculate oneself against the shock of leavetaking of power is by conducting a continuing series of self-assessments in which the perquisites of office are scrutinized and the power possessor is able to put it all into perspective. Among recent Presidents of the United States, Harry Truman was by far the least affected by the leaving of the office. Truman was a simple man, though not a simplistic one. People laughed at the story that he continued to wash his own socks in the White House. They relate the anecdote of Truman taking a visiting dignitary on a tour of the White House grounds. The VIP exclaimed at the greenness of the lawn. Truman responded enthusiastically, "The thing you have to do is get a big load of horse manure and rub it in, get right down there with your hands and rub it in." Margaret Truman and her mother were present. Margaret was appalled, and later she said so to her mother. Mrs. Truman answered, "If you only knew how long it has taken me to get him to say manure."

We can speculate that had Lincoln lived, he would have made the adjustment well (even allowing for the fact that the artifacts of prestige were far less grandiose in his day). There is the story of the leader of the French Chamber of Deputies, visiting Washington, who came upon the President shining his shoes. Shocked, the French notable could not help saying, "The Emperor of France does not shine his own shoes." Interested, Lincoln paused and asked, "Oh, no? Whose shoes does he shine?"

Consider a current relationship that gives you power— your job, your standing in the community, whatever. What do you really enjoy most about it? Chances are that upon due deliberation you will acknowledge that much of your joy derives from prestige, the details of recognition of your position. The Bible tells us that it is not money but the love of money that is the "root of all evil." So it is with power and prestige; the love of them is the curse.

Now, how much of that prestige has been earned by you, and how much "comes with the territory"? One way to answer would be by saying all of it has been earned, because, after all, you managed to achieve the position. This we might call the Richard M. Nixon approach. Nixon felt—and acted on the feeling—that the achievement of the presidency should give him limitless prestige, that the office should be sur- rounded by great pomp, and that all of this was his, Richard Nixon's, rather than something that accompanied the job no matter who was in it. His abortive effort to dress the White House Guard of Honor in Ruritanian musical-comedy costumes was one example. In *The Final Days* Woodward and Bernstein tell of an evening when the presidential yacht moored at Mount Vernon. On the bow the President and his aides stood while the ship's bells tolled, taps was played, a recording of the national anthem was broadcast. All of this ceremony was prescribed by Navy regulations. At the con- clusion the President said to James St. Clair, "They pay you nickels and dimes, but this is what makes it worth it." Alexan- der Haig and the others who heard this, say the authors, "looked away in embarrassed silence."

The embarrassment is natural, but there should be no surprise. Nixon was a man who went further than most in assuming the trappings of power to be his personal due, but he was by no means unique in his vulnerability to such seduction.

Note the parts of your relationship that are trappings. Separate out the real work—the thought, the decisions, the accomplishments. They are yours. Their effects will remain with you in terms of reputation, the regard of those qualified to judge your accomplishments (and this group is much smaller than the public at large) and the experiences and enhanced capacity that your work gives you.

The rest of it is show. Enjoy it. Use it as a relaxant and a means of rewarding yourself for care and effort. But do every- thing possible to keep it from becoming a part of you, or, more properly, from letting yourself become a part of it.

Think from time to time about the contingency that

all this may end very suddenly. Identify what will remain with you. You will have the memory of accomplishment and probably some pride in your successes. You will have the feeling, one hopes, of having used power wisely and for maximum good. And you will have grown; you will bring along enlarged capacities to your next stage of life.

But you will not bring the bells and the playing of the anthem. These are fickle sweethearts. Once you are out of the position they will be gone. Treat them as enjoyable but very transitory bits of pleasure. Keep them in perspective; be ready to say goodbye to them when they leave you. The essence of successful leavetaking of power is the constant recognition and self-reminder of what is real power and what is just the surrounding fanfare. We once asked a former governor of a large eastern state what it was like to have the bands playing, the salutes, the escorts, and everyone including the White House calling for advice. He said, "You must realize you are on a honeymoon. Enjoy it while you can, but don't take it seriously."

Taking leave of youth is something we all do. The only question is how we do it. We can be carried along by the current of the years, struggling and covering our eyes. Or we can swim with the current, finding our places in a new phase of life.

The first and most significant change will have to come from inside all of us as individuals. The treatment of the elderly will improve as it reflects new attitudes toward the aging process. We hear so much about our scandalous tendency to shut "senior citizens" away, out of sight, in inadequate institutions. What we really cannot stand is the sight of ourselves growing older, mirrored in the faces of those who have gotten there before us.

The process of managing the leavetaking from youth and vigor should begin early. The first principle is the simple, flat-out recognition of the inevitability of what is happening.

The end of aging is death. That's one of the reasons we don't like to see it, think about it, or admit that it has to happen. Instead of fighting off thoughts of aging and death, it can be useful to sit down and let oneself think, really think, about the ultimate. You will die; so will we. Let your mind dwell on this for a time. Don't pretty it up, don't sugarcoat it with occult visions of life beyond the grave unless you truly believe in them. Our burgeoning interest in the occult and all its facets is another manifestation of the widespread nature of this leavetaking crisis. It is harmless enough until it begins to sidetrack us from full utilization and enjoyment of all of the possibilities that growing maturity opens up for us.

For growing older *does* have its advantages. We learn as we grow. If we are wise and lucky, we learn more about how to accomplish and how to enjoy. The attributes of maturity open up possibilities for satisfaction that cannot be realized by the young no matter how strenuously they try. If we are negotiating this leavetaking properly, we grow not only older but broader and deeper. We learn to enjoy the pleasure of *slowness.* We savor the delights of life unavailable to those who speed past them in the search for the Fountain of Youth.

Once we accept the inevitability of the coming termination of the days of youth, we are ready to plan the leavetaking. It's important that we don't think of it as a sharp break. True, people do wake up on certain days and exclaim "I'm getting old!"—but this is a matter of sudden realization and not a true picture of what is happening. We are getting old right now. We are also gathering the resources that will make the next phase of life more satisfying—if we will only learn to use them.

Can we stay young? Are we "as young as we feel"?

Some people try to retain youth by acting young, being bold and innovative, engaging in strenuous physical activity, dressing and looking youthful. That's fine if you can do it. Not everyone can. The strain increases, and the effects can be ludicrous. This approach to youthfulness is "youth transmission." Those who adopt it are constantly sending a signal: "Don't let the years fool you; I am *young!*"

There may be a better way—the approach of youth *reception*. This means continuing open-mindedness and receptivity to new ideas. It means talking with young people and really listening to them without necessarily trying to compete with them. It means reactivation of youthful idealism within the framework of a mature perspective.

Youth *receptors* acknowledge the realities of time and change while remaining open and flexible. You may not be able to be a youth transmitter, but you can be a youth *receptor.*

# $X$ RETIREMENT ON THE JOB

LEAVETAKING from the job can be a big problem at the point of retirement. However, there are a great many people today who have in effect retired, but they are still officially in their jobs. Once their work was absorbing. Now they have taken leave of it in all of the aspects that gave them zest and drive, but they still struggle with the growing worries of keeping the job and coping with its ever more annoying details.

The on-the-job retiree goes through the motions. He—or she—comes to work every day. He assumes all of the outward trappings of the working function. But inside, nothing is happening.

In his mind he has quit. He probably does not realize it. He thinks, I'm a little tired, a little stale. He assumes that the difficulty is temporary. He pushes himself to struggle with things that were once second nature. He groans with boredom as he takes on chores that he previously tackled with optimism and high spirits.

This person is in a partial leavetaking situation similar to that of the individual who remains in a marriage when everything about the marriage is going sour. Most of the more malignant effects of leavetaking are present, but the situation is stalled. The parties involved are not moving toward a complete, positive leavetaking that will set up a progression into a new and satisfying phase. The leavetaking will come, all right, but it will be dragged out, painful and damaging to everyone.

The problem is becoming more prevalent, particularly among executives. The demands of management are complex and rigorous, making the lure of on-the-job retirement more powerful. Executive compensation plans, with assured retirement programs and deferred payment, appear to lessen the monetary necessity for continued peak performance. (When the crunch comes, however, the on-the-job retiree will find that he is in trouble.) There is a growing inclination to "enjoy life while you can." This is not in itself a bad idea. The trouble develops when the individual permits himself to indulge in pursuits that he really does not enjoy while slacking off on those that have offered him emotional sustenance.

The executive who has quit on the job is not at first all that easy to identify, either for himself or for others. But he manifests the one overriding characteristic: he appears to be more interested in enjoying power than in using it.

The person who has quit while still at work does not usually make the one major positive move that might constitute at least a partial benefit. He does not become more devoted to his family. No. He spends just as much time as he did before in job-connected situations, but what he does in those situations is different. He moves in and out of problem areas rather than sticking with them. He becomes pre-occupied with "busy work." Once he would identify a di-lemma, organize the attack on it, and follow through until something was accomplished. Now he holds a meeting or writes a memo, and then turns his back for a week or two while occupying himself with less important matters.

The on-the-job retiree travels a lot. Of course many executives have to travel a great deal, but they usually have good reasons for their trips. The executive dropout begins to jet around just for the sake of traveling. No jaunt is too point-less as long as it takes him away from the nagging problems of his *In* box. He becomes a compulsive attender of meetings and conventions, particularly if they take place in another location.

The person in this state of suspended leavetaking from working responsibilities is restless. Outside interests take up more of his time. He is unpredictable. Colleagues and sub-ordinates can't figure him out.

He is hard to reach. When he suspects that someone who wants to see him will raise difficult questions, he becomes altogether unavailable. When subordinates do win through to confront him, they find him bored, impatient with detail, anxious to terminate conversations. He avoids decisions. He changes the subject a lot. He reminisces.

This person is coasting. Superficially he may appear to be enjoying the fruits of the efforts that brought him to his present position. But he is not happy. He is trapped in a leavetaking situation that causes current pain and will lead to lasting damage.

A lot of the people who manifest these symptoms are victims of "middle-age megrims." They are beginning to wonder if it has All Been Worthwhile. They think back wistfully on alternate turnings that their lives might have taken—"I had a chance to be head of my own business and

I blew it!" They feel pushed by younger, hungrier tigers, and they find it difficult to muster up the energy to respond to the challenge.

A manager may have retired on the job for a long time before it begins to show. If he has been effective in the past he has built up an organization that can function, within limits, without him. Good subordinates tend to take on more responsibility—and this, at least, may be a good thing. As long as the organization's priorities remain valid, the machinery keeps on running. Results diminish, but so gradually that the erosion is hard to spot.

The on-the-job retiree does not realize what is happening to him; indeed, he is often the last to know. We can always find ways to rationalize waning interest and vigor.

As the international management consultant Henry Golightly points out, the effects set in insidiously and almost invisibly. Subordinates begin to spend more time figuring out how to work around the boss than work with him. They become accustomed to the idea that nobody is watching their performances very closely. Some start to probe, to find out just how far they can go on their own. Others are scared by their increased freedom. (All ambitious individuals assert that they yearn for greater latitude, but when it comes, many are afflicted with management agoraphobia.)

And inevitably the palace revolution begins to take shape. Nobody comes right out and says anything about it at first, but the notion spreads that the top man may be ripe for the plucking. The organization becomes involved in a ritual that traces back (as we can see in Frazer's *Golden Bough*) to time immemorial—the killing of the old king.

But the real trouble sets in when the time comes that the organization—a department, a division or an entire company —must reorder its priorities and strike out in new directions. As long as the unit has continued to move toward preset ob-

jectives that are still valid—even under slackened leadership
—things have gone along with some semblance of purpose
and impetus.

But change makes the need for new directions inevitable.
When the time comes, only the boss can give these new directions. Subordinates can advise, they can contribute, but they
cannot handle the task of reorientation. Leadership is vital;
and the executive dropout does not provide it.

Companies have failed because one or more key people
retired while still on the job. Many others are failing today
for the same reason. This is not a rare phenomenon; it happens all the time. And since the phenomenon encompasses
so many of the elements of leavetaking, we can see it more
clearly—and perhaps come up with some useful answers—
when we view on-the-job quitting as a leavetaking episode.

People who get into this kind of trouble are reluctant to
admit it to themselves, and reluctant to pull out of the job,
because they are afraid of the consequences of parting from
the job. This is true even when money is not the primary
factor. Leaving a job in which one has made real accomplishments and achieved real power is a scary proposition. There
is the unknown future looming darkly. And there is the
symbolism of actual quitting: the acknowledgment that a
phase of life is over. To admit that one can't do a job any
more is to admit that one is distinctly closer to death. The
difficulty is, however, that by failing to make the admission,
we condemn ourselves to a kind of death-in-life in which
we are trapped in an arid situation, the end of which is likely
to be a leavetaking that is forced on us.

For the individual who has a faint suspicion that he may
have retired on the job, or may be in the process of doing so,
the first essential consideration is to realize that he is by no
means unique. The manager who has reached the mid-forties
is not ready for the boneyard, but he is shortsighted if he
assumes he can maintain the same degree of physical and

mental vigor and adventurousness that he possessed fifteen years before.

No. The healthy personality is able to accommodate the process of growing older through a series of positive leave-takings. He graduates from those stages he has outgrown and moves into new stages. He enjoys new challenges and puts into play new strengths that he did not have fifteen years before to replace those he has lost. It's like a star big-league shortstop. He comes to the majors at twenty-two and achieves stardom because of his great speed and strength of arm. At thirty-five he is obviously not as fast, nor can he throw as hard. If he tries to kid himself that he is still able to measure up to the physical standards of more than a decade ago, he will be finished. He retains and even enhances his value now by replacing sheer physical ability with brains and experience. He knows the batters and where to play them. He covers his position by means of art rather than by pure physical vigor.

The person who has made his way up through drive, daring and boundless energy cannot continue to call on those attributes forever. They will fail him. He will grow frustrated and restless. He will quit on the job.

Look for the telltale signs of on-the-job retirement in yourself as well as in others. Spot the increasing tendency to become involved in peripheral activities, the urge to travel for the sake of traveling, the impatience with details, the unwillingness to make decisions, the tendency to make oneself unavailable. Sometimes the most significant indications may be found in the attitudes and actions of subordinates. Do people who once came to you for help now try to go it alone? Are there a great many unofficial rump sessions at which down-the-line personnel put their heads together to figure out ways to get things done? At meetings do people who once raised significant issues now merely go through the motions?

Sometimes executives try to combat staleness in themselves or in others through the application of dollars. But more money will not cure the ailment. Often it exacerbates the problem. The corporate dropout does not lose his drive because of lack of money. Indeed, if he is made to feel that he can make more money while reducing his involvement, he will withdraw further from engagement with the active challenges of the job.

Pride is a more useful key than money. A person who has accomplished things at work is proud of them. When he helps himself, or helps somebody else, to see that those accomplishments are being frittered away, he will be willing to seek ways to reverse the process of deterioration.

One course that offers real promise is that kind of "on-the-job leavetaking" in which the individual takes leave of the aspects of the work he has outgrown, shaves away the barnacles of routine that are holding him back. This need not mean moving to a new job. It can be done by shaking up the routine and by focusing on the important elements of the job.

When you feel yourself going stale, make an inventory of all of the aspects of the job. As we suggest elsewhere, develop an idea of the extent to which each aspect gives you fulfillment and makes demands on you. Look at the parts of the task that have become most distasteful. Are you still trying to do them in the same way you did before? How much can be changed? Can you take on these things at a different time of the day? Can you talk with different people about them? Instead of trying to grapple with several problems at once, can you devote an uninterrupted stretch to just one problem until you have solved it?

Look at your job as if you had just been called upon to invent it. Structure it from the ground up to suit you. Forget about the way you have been doing it. Concentrate on the objectives and then figure out the best and most satisfying means by which you can work toward those objectives *now*. If you do this with reasonable objectivity, you will come up with a different way of working. To some degree you will have rebuilt your relationship with the job. You will have broken with the past and formed a new kind of association that meets today's needs.

This is positive leavetaking.

# *XI* DEATH: THE LAST LEAVETAKING

IT IS VERY DIFFICULT to write—or read—about death with clinical objectivity, but it is important to try.

It is beyond the boundaries of our subject to consider the likelihood and the possible nature of life after earthly death, except to comment on the role that such belief may play in the handling of the trauma of the survivor.

Death *is* a leavetaking. It differs from other leavetakings in its awesome degree, not in its essential nature. People who manage well in the serious leavetakings of life acquire the maturity to face death with dignity and a measure of tranquility; and they are better able to deal with the deaths of those close to them.

When someone we love dies, all of the mechanisms of leavetaking come into play with an intensity unparalleled by any other experience. Object loss is deepened by the utter finality of the event. Role loss—"What will I do now?"—is magnified by despair. And the shock is made all the more severe by the inescapable resonances of our own final end. Donne's ominous words echo: "Never send to know for whom the bell tolls; it tolls for thee."

There are internal processes that go to work when someone close to us dies. They are painful. However, if we assist them, or at least do not impede them, these processes will enable us to surmount the shock and resume normal life. We can help to prepare ourselves by understanding what happens when we mourn.

The study of reaction to death began to develop as a branch of psychology about fifty years ago. Clinicians began to work toward identifying the combination of psychological and physical effects that is now known as the syndrome of acute grief. One extremely significant contribution was made by E. Lindemann, who studied survivors of those who died in the fire that swept the Cocoanut Grove nightclub in Boston on November 28, 1942, killing 491 people.*

As a result of this work we now know that acute grief is a distinct syndrome; that the syndrome may appear immediately upon the heels of the loss, may be delayed or exaggerated, or may be apparently absent. An example of this is the situation in which a child seems to respond to the death of his father with near indifference. Six months later, when his cat dies, he is totally bereft.

There are six stages of grief: shock and disbelief; developing awareness; restitution; resolving loss; idealization; outcome.

In the initial stage, shock and disbelief, we refuse to accept the fact of loss. We shut our eyes and turn off our psychic hearing aids. In the second stage the reality of the loss begins

* E. Lindemann, "Symptomatology and the Management of Acute Grief," *American Journal of Psychiatry*, 101:141, 1944.

to penetrate. Feelings of emptiness and anguish rush in. The bereaved person may become angry, feel that he has somehow failed. There is impulsive "acting-out" behavior.

In the third stage, restitution, the work of mourning is assisted by the rites and customs surrounding the funeral. The living go through a ritualized form of restitution which also serves to knot them together again.

The fourth stage is resolving the loss. Here the bereaved begins to deal with role loss as against object loss. Sometimes the activity is appropriate, sometimes not. For example, survivors may become extremely concerned with their own health and overprotective of their own loved ones.

Then comes the step of idealization, in which negative feelings and hostility toward the dead person are repressed. This is a particularly dangerous stage. One study observes that "the friend will often either sever other close relationships because he cannot handle another potential loss or he will try to rekindle ex-friendships in which he believes he committed a similar act of unkindness."

In the final stage the survivors are able to remember and talk about the dead person with a measure of objectivity, remembering the bad things as well as the good ones, often with a tinge of humor. This kind of reminiscence is frequently considered to be the province of the family. The friend who tries to join is turned away. One will see at an Irish wake several close relatives exchanging stories, sometimes ribald ones, about the deceased. A friend stands listening. Finally he comes forth with his own recollections. The reaction is cool; there is only perfunctory response. The group dissolves.

Throughout there is pain. Winston Churchill said, "Physical wounds at the time of receipt are amazingly endurable. Only later do they hurt, smart and burn. So it is with the major losses of life."

All of this supports the vital point that one of the most

insidious things about grief is that there is frequently no acceptable way of demonstrating it. When sadness for any loss is discouraged, the work of mourning is circumvented. We must find ways to work out our losses.

Doctors used to sedate people suffering from acute grief; many still do. But there is a growing feeling that this is the wrong approach. Elisabeth Kubler-Ross suggests instead that the hospital should furnish a "screaming room" to which the bereaved can repair to weep and moan. The point is that ventilation of the grief is healthier than repression.

There is a universal tendency to deny loss. When a loved one dies, survivors often cannot believe that the death has occurred, thus impelling certain psychic mechanisms to operate as if indeed it had not taken place. Physicians and psychologists are now alert to the dangers in this tendency. Robert G. Twycross remarks that he almost always asks whether the bereaved want to see the body before it is taken to the morgue. About two-thirds say they would like to. He quotes a survivor's typical response: "If I hadn't seen him myself . . . I don't think I would believe that he's dead." Twycross adds, "One of the most important functions of wakes, funerals and burials is not to call to mind for the bereaved that a reality is occurring or has occurred, but to provide crucial opportunities for reality testing to take place during the time of acute grief."*

Bereavement may bring with it a curious possessiveness. When the Spanish painter Juan Gris died in 1927 Gertrude Stein was devastated. Gris was a close friend, but, more than that, she considered him to be her special discovery. She had bought his paintings early, when no one else was buying them, and it seemed to her that she had always supported the Spaniard when he was totally rejected by the rest of the world. This was not altogether true. Stein had supported Gris when

* Robert G. Twycross, "Acute Grief: A Physician's Viewpoint," in Pine *et al.*, *op. cit.*

he needed money; in return she had received paintings at low prices. The relationship had ended in some bitterness.

But objective fact is masked by selective perception at death. Stein's reaction is described by Janet Hobhouse: "So possessive of Gris was Gertrude that when Picasso, who she thought had always been jealous of Gris, came to the Rue de Fleurus to talk about his death, Gertrude had attacked him. As she tells the story in *The Autobiography of Alice B. Toklas:* 'Gertrude Stein said to him bitterly, You have no right to mourn, and he said, You have no right to say that to me. You never realized his meaning because you did not have it, she said angrily.' "*

There often is a pecking order in mourning. The closest relatives of the dead person are tacitly assumed to be "entitled" to harbor greater grief than those whose relationship is not as close, or who are merely friends. Among the Orthodox Jews this order is formalized. During the Kaddish, or prayer for the dead, only the immediate kin are permitted to stand. (Reformed Jews all stand for the Kaddish.) It is natural in all cultures for close relatives of the departed to look askance at someone less close who seems to be mourning more deeply, or at least more evidently. Such things are not done. Long after the funeral is over they may be remembered and resented.

This makes it difficult for friends and distant relatives. They may be hit just as hard by the death—but they have fewer mechanisms to call upon with which to do the work of mourning. When a close relative wails and erupts in anger, it may be embarrassing but it is acceptable. When a friend does it he is regarded as an exhibitionist or an eccentric.

It is permissible to grieve deeply and publicly at the death of a member of the family. It is not permissible (for others or

* Janet Hobhouse, *Everybody Who Was Anybody* (New York: Putnam's, 1975).

for oneself) to grieve deeply over the death of a dog or cat or the junking of an old piece of furniture. It is not permissible to grieve at all over the cancellation of a favorite television show. And yet we often feel like grieving over trivialities; and indeed we are grieving.

The problem of the lack of adequate opportunities for mourning may have political, cultural and social aspects. When Tom Mboya, Minister for Defense in Kenya, was assasinated, he was buried, according to custom, on his father's land, with only members of his own tribe attending. This excluded many people, particularly among the Kikuyus. The difficulty was exacerbated by the fact that a member of the Kikuyu tribe had killed Mboya. Prevented from expressing their grief and guilt formally, these people erupted in violence.

Many of those close to the scene have been concerned for a long time about what may happen when Jomo Kenyatta, the present President of Kenya, dies. Mr. Kenyatta is a Kikuyu. Members of the Luo, the second most powerful tribe in Kenya, may be excluded from the ceremonies. If this happens, there may be a devastating reaction.

In this connection we may note the events following the assassination of Dr. Martin Luther King, Jr. Dr. King's funeral was a national event, seen on television by millions. Leaders from various segments of the society participated. It was thus possible for millions to share in the proceedings and to ventilate, at least to some degree, their feelings. This fact appears to have been a major element in defusing the potentially explosive situation created by Dr. King's murder.

The funeral provides the framework for support that the bereaved person needs in the struggle back toward normality.

Dr. Robert Fulton interviewed 565 widows and widowers and found that "the people who participated in what would be termed a 'traditional' funeral, i.e. who viewed the body and who involved their friends and relatives in the ceremony, reported having fewer adjustment problems than those who did not." Those who had a "regular" funeral retained more positive thoughts about the dead person. Moreover, the funeral seems to have brought the family closer together. (Here we might ask which came first, the funeral or the warm feelings? It may be that people who are disposed to feel this way are people who tend to have funerals.)

One other observation by Dr. Fulton is worth noting. In the group he studied, wives arranged earth burials for their husbands. However, "husbands, particularly those reporting a professional occupation, had their wives' bodies cremated in a significantly greater number of instances."* It would be perilous to speculate on this. We might add, though, that this group, the cremators, reported the least positive memory of the deceased and the greatest difficulty in adjusting.

Mourning is ambivalent. We must banish the dead person and incorporate him at the same time.

Western culture, in its emphasis on "taking it like a man," inhibits us by suggesting that we should not show emotions. The notion of "taking it like a man" is, of course, also virulently sexist. It is all right for women to weep, but not men. In this respect, unlike most others, the sexist attitude has probably worked to the benefit of women in that they are under far less pressure to internalize grief.

Funeral customs in most societies involve some kind of expenditure, whether it be in goods, services or money. If it costs us something, our guilt is somewhat assuaged. Of course if this were truly an effective mechanism, the most expensive undertakers would be the greatest benefactors of mankind.

Indeed, when the loss is trivial, or is of a nature that is perceived as trivial, it may be more difficult to get over it.

---

* Robert Fulton, in Pine *et al., op. cit.*

Mourning the death of a loved one is acceptable. Mourning the loss of a shirt is not. Nevertheless there are cases in which the loss of the shirt may hurt as much, because it triggers repressed reactions to other losses.

Losses confront us with intimations of our own mortality. They make us sad, angry, bewildered—to an extent. We try to temper our reactions according to the "social value" of the loss (for example, a death weighs more than a job, a job weighs more than a shirt). We may dismiss the griefs of children because we know they are ill-founded.

But tempering the reaction does not dispel the possibility of psychic damage. On the contrary, it may exacerbate it.

From our observations of death we may extract some principles that apply to all loss situations:

Mourning is a therapeutic process.

The grief is not the trauma. Grief is a healing agent. It is the psychic white corpuscles that counteract the virus of leavetaking trauma.

We need to be able to express our feelings about loss.

Repression of grief is harmful.

Grief must be public to be shared and shared to be diminished.

We often idealize the lost object.

Leavetaking involves two elements: role loss and object loss.

At some point we must accept the reality of the loss.

The possibility of leavetaking trauma is heightened when we do not have adequate means of grieving.

What emerges from this is the truth that the pain caused by the death of a loved one is great but not irrevocable.

When we begin to ask, "What do I do now?" we have begun the essential process of moving on to the next stage. We will experience relapses. We will be lonely. We will sometimes be torn between the mourning behavior that is expected of us and the way in which we must work out our own grief.

If we have developed an understanding of leavetaking, and if we have been able to manage other leavetakings, we can handle this one. And in the end we will be able to face our own death with fortitude and serenity.

# *XII*  IT HURTS—AND IT SHOULD


THE FIRST REACTION to an abrupt leavetaking is chaotic—a welter of rage, shock, fear, guilt. You are in an emotional storm. Mariners know that when a typhoon strikes, the greatest danger is that the ship will "broach to"—come broadside to the waves. When this happens the vessel no longer answers the helm. The wind and sea take command, and the ship is in deadly peril of sinking or capsizing.

To try to run before the storm is to increase the danger. The only hope is to heave to and ride it out. "Heaving to" means keeping just enough way on to keep the bow headed into the wind. The huge waves wash over the decks and superstructure, but the ship can survive.

In the immediate emotional storm of critical leavetaking the best policy in the first moments may be to ride it out. Don't try to make important decisions or follow a course. Heave to and let the waves break over you.

The waves of pain are hard to handle, but it is better to

suffer them than to try to avoid them, either by fleeing or by excessive self-sedation. Just keep enough "way" on to ride the storm.

Most things in life have some useful purpose, even pain. Pain is a warning to the organism (albeit a late-acting one) that danger is imminent. It is a medium for learning. The cat that has jumped onto a hot stove will not jump onto a hot stove again. (One commentator has observed that the cat will not jump onto a cold stove either, but this is a slander on cats; the cat responds to the heat, not the stove.)

And pain—as in the discomfort associated with high body temperature—is a signal that the organism is responding to combat something that is harmful to it.

Leavetaking causes pain. The psychic distress we feel when we say goodbye is not merely a superficial element of the process. It is more than a symptom. It is an integral part of the work of healing.

One of the problems that modern society has failed to solve is not the problem of pain but rather the problem of *avoidance* of pain. Previous generations lived with the fatalistic certainty that pain is a part of life. You could not avoid a certain measure of it, so you had to endure it.

Nowadays a lot of us see it differently. We have grown to accept the proposition that it is possible to live out our lives altogether free of suffering if we are just smart enough and rich enough to do so. It is thought dumb to accept pain. Consequently we have become enormously resourceful in avoiding pain, and have devised sophisticated means, external and internal, for doing so.

Medical and psychiatric practitioners are alarmed at the consequences of the concept that complete absence of suffering is the desired norm, and that all pain can, and should, be avoided. They see how our efforts to avoid distress in the short run do great damage in the long run. The problem is made worse by the apparent success of the pain-evading mechanisms that human beings have developed.

There are a number of ways in which we can try—and often seem to succeed—to make leavetaking a painless process. For example, one method is denial.

Another way in which we attempt to evade the pain of departure is by transferring it to somebody else. Many leavetakings cause anger, which is a natural reaction. Sometimes the bereaved intensifies his anger and focuses it on one particular person or entity. When one is entirely absorbed in acting out rage, no matter how illogical or poorly aimed that rage may be, consciousness of personal pain may seem to be diminished. The exercise of the rage reaction can be carried to fantastic lengths. A man is fired by a company. He devotes his time thereafter—until he is caught—to planting bombs at the company's facilities. Most individuals do not have to come anywhere close to becoming "mad bombers" to go to unhealthy extremes in trying to transfer pain. Many people go on for years obsessed with anger as the result of a leavetaking experience.

Another device for avoiding pain is withdrawal. Confronted by the distress of parting, we retreat from life. The bereaved person sits and broods. He says little, does nothing. He has retreated into a cave. Since each contact with the world—with people, places and things—seems to revive the pain, the major aim in life becomes the avoidance of those occasions of renewed distress.

Some people attempt to blot out pain by resorting to the principle of the counterirritant. This is the idea of widely marketed "painkilling" salves and lotions. You have an ache in your back, so you rub on a preparation to stop it. The stuff you rub on does not really kill the pain. On the contrary, it generates heat and thus produces pain. But the added pain seems to diffuse the initial agony, and the patient feels better.

Bereaved people, suffering the single sharp pain of loss, may seek out other pains. They stop taking care of themselves. They make themselves sick, so sick that the new and broader pain engulfs and appears to blot out the initial agony. This is a singularly dangerous course of action, physically and psychically.

And then, of course, there are drugs. At the first twinge we are conditioned to pop a pill. Aspirin is old hat; we see commercials in which the kindly fellow behind the drugstore counter assures the inquiring customer that this product is *really* strong.

We have trouble sleeping after a loss? We take sleeping pills. We feel depressed? We take an "upper." In physical terms this is a most dangerous thing, because the painkillers really do eliminate the pain. Since the pain is a signal that something is wrong, the recourse to a painkiller is like disconnecting all the fire alarms in a building where a fire has begun in the basement. The star fullback of the football team can hardly walk, his ankle hurts so much. The coach fixes him up by bestowing on him enough pills to cover the palm of one hand. The fullback plays the game and is crippled for life.

Recourse to pills and alcohol as painkillers is one of the more common and insidious forms of avoidance of the distress of leavetaking.

When we go to extremes to avoid the pain of bereavement we abort the work of healing. The really sinister element is that these techniques for dodging distress are most harmful when they seem to work best. If denial of loss creates an illusion of pain-free existence, the psyche is inclined toward continuance of the denial. The same is true of the counter-irritant, or the transfer of pain, or withdrawal from the occasions of pain. These evasive tactics may be as habit-forming as drugs or alcohol.

Disbelief, anger and depression are all parts of the necessary psychic healing process. They are stages through which we must pass if we are to safeguard ourselves against permanent trauma. By going all out to stop the pain at one particular stage, we may seem to succeed. But we may also stop the process. We freeze ourselves in a phase of mourning. Once frozen, we stick there, unable to move out of the past and grow into a new and ultimately rewarding stage of life.

### Giving Yourself Time to Grieve

There's an old music-hall song that goes something like this:

> From sport to sport they hurry me
> To stifle my regret
> They cosset me and flurry me
> And think that I forget.

It's great to have friends when you are suffering from the effects of a critical leavetaking. But sometimes your friends are not really helpful. The more attentive they are, the more they may contribute to your problem.

Ben Scholl's wife suddenly left him and went off to Los Angeles with another man. Ben's friends have risen to the occasion. One or another calls early in the morning—would he like a ride to work? On the job he is by himself only in the men's room. His colleagues seem to find endless pretexts to talk with him, about business, baseball, TV, politics, the state of the world in general. The only things they never talk about are marriage, love and loss. Ben has a lunch date every day. After work he can choose among invitations to dinner; the one option that does not seem open is for him to eat by himself. Then at night people drop by to talk with him until it's time to go to bed. They take turns doing it.

Ben's friends are acting from what they think are the best possible motives. They have made a tacit agreement that the important thing is not to let him alone, because he will brood over the bereavement. And Ben goes along with it. He knows his friends mean well. Sometimes he has a very strong urge to be left alone, but at the same time he has the feeling that this would be bad for him.

So the only time that Ben Scholl is by himself to think about what has happened is the middle of the night. (He has even received indirect offers from would-be sleeping companions who could take care of that period.) Ben is not sleeping well. He does lie awake, brooding. And somehow the solicitous attentions of his friends do not seem to be working. Ben is getting worse, not better. He doesn't talk much. He looks terrible. He can't seem to concentrate on anything. So his friends redouble their efforts to stay with him, cheer him up, get his mind onto other things.

When we experience disruptive change—like critical leavetaking—we need some time to ourselves. We need a moratorium on other business. To brood? Yes. To think about the past? Yes. To be angry and sad? Yes. To mourn? Yes.

Left by ourselves during the period immediately following a serious bereavement, we are likely to do all those things. But at the same time we are doing something else. We are repairing the thread of continuity in our lives.

A healthy psyche will repair that damaged or broken thread. The work of mourning is necessary to the process. But to do this the mind needs emotional resiliency. When we are constantly involved with other people and forced to think about other things, the work of mourning is delayed. Furthermore, our emotional resiliency—already low—is exhausted. The bereaved person who is distracted all day long will go through the work of mourning only in the late hours of night—Scott Fitzgerald's "dark night of the soul, when it is always three o'clock in the morning."

Even when friends are not rallying round constantly, we resist giving ourselves over to the solitary process of grieving. We clean the house. We throw ourselves into our work. We seek companionship. We join the crowd. We go to bars and drink.

We have bought the idea that "brooding is the worst thing you can do." It is a confession of weakness; strong people (and we all want to be strong) don't mourn. It is unhealthy; brooding will just make things worse. It is painful; we look for the opiate that will stave off the pain, whether that opiate takes the form of activity, companionship, alcohol or drugs. And mourning is an affront to our friends, who wish us well and who are trying so hard to cheer us up.

Friends hurry us "from sport to sport" because they want to help. There may be other reasons, subconscious ones— guilt and fear. Sometimes the most solicitous friend is acting out a deep-seated feeling that he has not done enough. Sometimes he is responding to a kind of superstitious revulsion from sadness or even thoughtfulness. Shakespeare's Caesar said, "Let me have men about me that are fat; Sleek-headed men, and such as sleep o' nights." The attentive friend may be guilty about his own ambiguous reaction to your troubles. La Rochefoucauld remarks that "In the adversity of our best friends we often find something that is not exactly displeasing."

And then our friends want to measure up in the crisis because they wish to prove their steadfastness. They are aware that the time is apt to come when the bereaved one looks back and reflects: When something like that happens you find out who your real friends are. The "real friends" are the ones who were constantly rallying round.

And yet it is often the person who is willing to let you alone for a while who will do you the most good.

There is no way to escape the grief of leavetaking. By trying to escape it, or repress it, or direct our minds away from it, we can only make sure that we suffer all of the negative effects of mourning without benefiting from the positive ones.

When you are hit by a leavetaking, give yourself some time alone. Mourn; let the process go forward, and let it go forward at a time when you have some emotional strength, not at three o'clock in the morning. In doing your mourning, don't allocate your time according to some externally imposed idea of the proper period that you may take. Sometimes people act as if there were a sliding scale of mourning: a year for the death of a husband or wife, ten months for a parent, eight months for a divorce, six months for a separation— down to thirty seconds for a pair of cuff links. It doesn't work that way. The loss that seems trivial according to conventional standards may hit us harder than what is assumed to be a major blow. It may resonate with associations that we do not recognize. And our difficulties with mourning over what others see as a minor matter are made worse because we are not reacting in a way that is socially appropriate.

Give yourself the time alone you need. Tell the solicitous friend, "I appreciate what you're doing. But I do need to be alone. I am not going to cut my wrists. I need to think. I will feel better after it."

By getting off by yourself—for a time—you are not only doing the natural thing; you are doing the healthy thing.

THE TRAP OF DENIAL: IT
DIDN'T HAPPEN

THE CENTRAL FIGURE of William Faulkner's "A Rose for Emily" is a proper southern spinster. Many years in the past, when Miss Emily was young, black-haired and beautiful, she had a beau, a dashing young man who had come into town and swept Miss Emily off her feet. There were those who called him a rake and a ne'er-do-well. But Miss Emily was in love with him. They were to be married. The night before the wedding day the young man disappeared, never to be seen again. Since that night Miss Emily has been alone. Nobody goes to see her.

Miss Emily dies. In her house there is only one bed. In the bed they find a man's skeleton. Next to the skull is a pillow with a depression as if another head has rested there. On the pillow there is a strand of gray hair.

Denial of loss, carried to a grotesque extreme.

Denial is not abnormal. When we lose something, we have

a tendency toward disbelief. Sometimes we act out that disbelief, behave as if the loss had not happened. The acting-out
phase is usually brief. Furthermore, it is only partial. Typically, the person who has suffered the loss acts out denial in
words: "It can't be true . . . I don't believe it . . . This can't
really be happening." Underneath, however, there is acknowledgment of the fact.

When the work of mourning operates normally, denial is
soon replaced by awareness of reality and behavior that con-
forms to reality. Rogers has been fired. He says to himself, "I
can't believe it." Nevertheless he clears out his desk, picks
up his final check, begins to think, however chaotically and
ineffectually, about the task of finding another job and the
mechanics of living until that other job is found.

But sometimes we remain too long in the denial phase,
and give ourselves over to it too fully. Denial becomes delu-
sion. Extreme denial is Scarlett O'Hara refusing to face the
fact that Rhett Butler is really gone, saying, "I'll think about
that tomorrow," but not thinking about it tomorrow.

Eve and Ken had lived together for two years. Ken walked
out six weeks ago. There was no scene; Eve said very little.
But since then Eve has, to the utmost degree possible, behaved as if it had not happened. She follows the old routine.
A couple of times a week—say, Tuesday and Thursday—
they went out to eat. A couple of times a week Eve eats alone
in the same places. On the nights when they didn't go out
she cooks the same meals and eats them by herself. Ken and
Eve used to go to the zoo on weekends, or ride bikes, or visit
museums. Eve continues to do these things. She tries to spend
her time as the two of them did, with the same schedule and
frequency. Sometimes Eve's presence is embarrassing to their
mutual friends. They don't know what to say. They don't
want to make things worse. Just after the break Ken would
be in some of the places that Eve kept going back to. No
more; Ken has changed his pattern to avoid seeing her. But

Eve goes on. She even watches the television shows that Ken watched and which she detested. She is silent and depressed.

Excessive denial of loss is usually caused by two factors acting in combination: guilt and fear.

*Guilt.* "The leavetaking is my fault. I am to blame. But I am not that bad a person. I can't be that bad a person. I cannot accept myself if I am that bad a person. But the loss proves that I am that bad a person. Therefore I will not accept the loss. If I act as if it did not happen, then it did not happen."

You may or may not be principally at fault. In any leavetaking, responsibility rarely rests solely on one side. But your guilt or lack of guilt is not an issue. We are not discussing that.

You have mixed up *acknowledgment* with *acceptance*. To acknowledge that something has happened is not to accept that it was right that it should happen, or that it was inevitable, or that you are to blame. Acknowledgment simply means: I see reality. The implications of that reality I may know later, when the dust settles. I may not know them at all. It may be altogether unimportant whether I know them or not.

If it is important to you to determine the degree of guilt, then the first step is to acknowledge the loss. You are putting yourself on trial. You will be judge and jury. The first step in any trial is always the establishment of the fact that a crime has, indeed, taken place.

*Fear.* "What I had and have lost was part of my armor. I was used to it, and to be used to something is to be safe. Leavetaking leaves me exposed to danger. *What do I do now?* I don't know. The best thing would be that if the loss hadn't happened. If I proceed as if it did not happen, I will be safe."

Fear of new situations is not abnormal. It becomes abnormal when it makes us do inappropriate things. To deny reality is a most inappropriate and dangerous thing. Only human beings do this. We say that the ostrich tries to hide from danger by burying its head in the sand. This is a myth we have built upon our own tendency to deny reality. What the ostrich actually does when confronted with a threat is quite appropriate behavior. It lowers its beak and elevates its tail. To a predator the ostrich then resembles a bush, from even a short distance away.

Loss is not in itself danger unless you make it so. A leave-taking is often the opposite of a threat. It is a part of growth, a progression from a lower state of maturity into a higher one.

The loss you have experienced may or may not carry danger with it. At the beginning you cannot tell. The only way that you can tell is by clearing your eyes so that you can look around and see whether the new situation offers threat or promise. Probably it offers a combination of both. To clear your eyes you must acknowledge reality. You have to say, *"It happened."* And you have to behave in conformity with your acknowledgment that it has happened.

We can offset excessive denial by preparing for loss.

Preparation is a matter of alternates. It is more than occasional idle speculation along the lines of "nothing goes on forever." It is active consideration, and perhaps testing out, of alternate modes of behavior that will be possible, and maybe necessary, when loss comes.

In her two years with Ken, Eve permitted the relationship to become, first, a routine, and then an all-encompassing, rigid way of life. Routine is insidious. It is comforting. We can grow overly dependent on it.

Go back to the beginning of Eve and Ken. Instead of gearing every activity to the relationship, let's suppose that Eve did certain things differently. Occasionally she takes the initiative in breaking the routine. She says, "No, let's not do that tonight. Let's do something different." Now and then she gets off by herself, with other friends, doing other things, without Ken.

Eve is preparing for possible loss. She is establishing in her mind the certainty that another mode of behavior is possible. She is permitting herself to try out alternate activities. She is establishing, or reestablishing, herself as an independent human being, who does not live only by rote. She is building resources that may be needed, rather than letting them lie dormant to atrophy. And, incidentally, by doing this Eve may also be safeguarding the relationship. The exploration of alternate modes of behavior by people who are close to each other is often one of the surest ways to keep that closeness alive. Bonds between people should remain supple and flexible. When they turn brittle and rigid they snap.

What are the factors you rely on most in your life? Think about them. Perhaps list them: the persons you spend the most time with, the activities that give you most pleasure, the places you enjoy, the possessions you have come to take for granted. Now take all of these factors and subtract them from your life. Unthinkable? Admittedly it is difficult, but it should not be unthinkable. There danger lies. The adage that nothing is permanent in life is a truism because it is true.

Husbands and wives can go away, or get sick, or die. Lovers can fall out of love. Jobs can be lost. Possessions can be lost. Children leave home. The capacity to enjoy sports or hobbies may disappear. We may have to move away from places we have gotten used to and come to love.

When you find a life factor that is particularly difficult to subtract from your conception of future existence, don't turn away from it. This is the focal point on which to concentrate in preparing for possible loss, because this is the factor that you are most likely to deny if and when it changes or disappears.

Fantasize. Build in your mind an existence *without* this key factor. Eve thinks, If Ken were not with me, what would I do? The time to think about this is when the desired object is fully with you, when it is in no danger. The solid security of its presence should make it possible for you to think objectively about the possibility of its absence. So think about it. At first your mind will slide away from the subject. Drop it; but come back to it.

Ask yourself, *"To what extent am I a complete human being?"* If your life contains a factor without which you could not function, you are not a complete human being. The factor has become a habit, a crutch. You are hooked on it.

Habits can be broken. The best way is through replacement, and elsewhere in this book we talk about that. In this context it is sufficient to recognize that a person, place, thing or state of existence can become a habit, like drugs, and that the withdrawal symptoms, in their own way, may be just as severe.

Who and what are you hooked on? Once you have isolated the factor, begin to reduce your dependence. If it is a person, spend some time away from that person, thinking and doing for yourself. If it is an object, deliberately do without that object for a bit. If it is a routine, occupational or recreational, shake up the routine.

Face the possible leavetaking, think of the alternative way of life that will be mandatory (there are always alternatives, often better than the original), and test it out. In this way, when the time of leavetaking arrives, you will not be so shaken that you are thrown into a state of protracted denial of reality.

Moreover, by exploring the alternatives now, you open for yourself the option of a leavetaking that is initiated by you rather than having to experience a loss that is forced on you. This does not mean that you decide now to take leave, only that you open your mind to the possibility. It may well be that in the far or near future you will find that there are compelling objective reasons for you to make the decision to leave. But if you are hooked and have never conceived of leaving the object, you will not leave, no matter how good it may be for you to do so.

### First Aid

It happens. You have not prepared, or even given it any thought. You lose something—human or otherwise—on which much of your existence has centered.

What to do?

*Step 1.* Do not hold back from grieving. Grieve *intensely.* Cry. Push yourself to feel all the pain.

But give yourself a limit. Let it all hang out, all your bereavement. Tell yourself, "This is my period for mourning my loss." Try to set a time limit for your intense grieving.

*Step 2.* In order to help yourself face reality, *accentuate* your dependence on the lost object. Your denial of reality is, after all, game-playing. Try to play the game to the full. You are Eve, going to the same places she went to with Ken, doing the things she did with him. You say to yourself, "I am actually *here* with Ken. He is physically at my side. I can reach out and touch him." But you can't, of course. He's not there. *That* you can acknowledge.

Having acknowledged that, you move on to the corollary. By denying the reality of the loss, you have been saying, "I cannot live without him, so he is not gone." But not only must you admit that he is not there, you must also admit that you *are* living, however miserable you may be.

Now we are moving into a different phase. You no longer deny that leavetaking has happened. You admit that it has happened. Now you are ready to act on that acknowledgment. The work of mourning is by no means over, but we have surmounted an important hurdle.

# *XIV* DENIAL II: IT HAPPENED, BUT WHO CARES?

ONE FORM OF DENIAL is to think and act as if the leavetaking had not taken place. In a variant form of denial the individual acknowledges the leavetaking but denies that the association was of any importance.

Mike Glenn used to bowl with the guys from work two nights a week. Other nights he drank beer with them. The gang ate lunch together. They were a closely knit group. Sometimes they would all get tickets to the hockey game, eat dinner beforehand, have a few drinks afterward.

One day at work Mike heard several of the men talking about the game they'd seen the night before. He hadn't been invited. A couple of weeks later, when they were getting up the teams for the new bowling season, Ted Beckerman, who was more or less the unofficial leader of the group, told Mike that the fellows wanted to do it differently this time. They were tired of always having the same guys on a team; things were getting into a rut. Why not split up, bring in some new bowlers, "change their luck"? Mike didn't see the point in this; he was not at all unhappy with the old way. But from what Ted said, everybody else felt this way, so Mike would have to go along. Ted added that he or somebody else would be talking to Mike in the next few days about what team he'd be on. Nobody talked to Mike, and within the month he discovered that the bowling arrangement was going to go on pretty much the way it had before—except that he was left out.

And so on. Mike Glenn was being shut out of the group. Reasons? Hard to say. It might have had something to do with work. Mike had had some differences with a few of the boys, including Ted. The problem had slopped over into union meetings. Nothing serious, Mike had thought, and anyway, he knew these guys well enough to be able to speak his mind about things, didn't he?

But Mike Glenn did not spend any time wondering about what had happened or trying to find out if anything was wrong. His response: "They don't want me to bowl with them? Who gives a damn? I don't need them anyway." Glenn took to elaborating this by telling himself that he had really been getting bored stiff with his companions: "They're all a bunch of dummies. Hanging out with them was a waste of time. Anyway, I didn't spend all that much time with them. Sure, you have a drink or two, kill a few minutes. But it didn't mean anything."

The unaccountable closing of ranks against one individual is a commonplace of childhood. The kid who is closed out doesn't know why it happens. The kids who do the closing out often don't know why either. It happens, and the reaction of the "outsider" is often to pretend that it doesn't make any difference. Childhood is full of these unthinking cruelties and these stoical reactions to unhappiness.

Indeed, "shutting out" is commonplace among all animals.

The pack closes ranks against one member. The outcast attempts to rejoin. Driven off, it will sometimes manifest what seems to be a "Who cares?" attitude.

Some grown-ups who are hit with an involuntary leavetaking avoid the trap of denying that it happened, but they fall into the trap of acting and *thinking* as if it meant nothing, as if there were no relationship there in the first place.

When we deny the magnitude of a strong relationship that has ended, we can often do a skillful acting job. We comport ourselves with every outward sign that the episode makes no difference. Furthermore, our role playing is good enough to convince certain parts of the mind. We begin to *think* that there was nothing there. Since the association meant nothing, then there is no disappointment, no frustration, no wishing that things were different, no pain.

The trouble with this is that it does not go deep enough to erase the memory of the relationship from all of the parts of the psyche. There remain considerable areas of our being in which pain *is* felt. The psychological situation is analogous to that of the patient who has lost a leg through amputation but who continues to feel that it is there.

When a relationship has been an involving one, denial of that involvement keeps the person from making a clean break with a situation that no longer exists. The umbilicals no longer function, but they have not been severed. We are bonded to a dead entity, and the fetters prevent us from forming fresh associations that will offer new satisfactions.

Mike Glenn makes some halfhearted passes at forming new friendships, but he does not really make new friends. He could manage to hook up with another bowling team, but that would mean running into the guys he used to bowl with. Now, since he is acting as if his friendship with the old bunch made no difference to him, he should not be hampered by the possibility of such an encounter. But of course it *did* make a difference. By failing to come to grips with the fact that a relationship of importance has ended, he has placed himself in a state of psychic suspension which precludes meaningful new action.

Glenn thinks he is going on as if nothing had happened. He doesn't realize the extent to which he has become morose, taciturn and touchy. His wife has noticed the change; his children feel it. The people who work with him are finding him harder to get along with. The truth that *something has happened* is manifest to all, except Mike.

Understand that when a relationship is broken, you will have a tendency to deny it. Sometimes that will take the form of denying that it happened. Sometimes it will consist in admitting that it happened but living in the fiction that it is of no importance. This is not the same thing as acknowledging the loss and its magnitude but pretending that it didn't make any difference. A person may choose to *pretend* to be unconcerned—and know that he is pretending. This may or may not be a wise course. It can have a social value in making one a more pleasant companion. The individual who chooses to act relatively untouched by leavetaking can be better company than one who is brooding all the time.

Denial II is different. Here the person tries to convince himself, not just others, that the former involvement meant nothing. The more successful you are in selling this bill of goods to yourself, the more trouble you may be storing up for yourself.

Face up to what you are losing when an association breaks off. Force yourself to admit that it did mean something. Zero in on the elements of the relationship that meant the most to you: companionship; support; occupation of time; security; love. When you do this—and only when you do it —will you be ready to move into the next phase, that of forming a new association that gives you what you need.

# *XV* THE TRAP OF "WHAT DOES IT MEAN?"

WE ARE ALWAYS ASKING "What does it mean?" Whether we are conscious of it or not, we look for the meaning behind the things that happen to us. This is how we struggle to keep our hold on life. Peter Marris (*Loss and Change,* Pantheon, 1974) calls this the *conservative impulse,* "an intolerance of unintelligible events." We are able to handle varying circumstances because we *impose* meaning on events. Often the meaning we impose contradicts the facts, but that does not stop us. As Marris points out, this imposition of meaning "does not always work, and it does not work for anyone all the time." We do it nevertheless because something inside us forces us to do it.

We are particularly anxious to impose on serious setbacks and painful events. Ancient tribes attributed eclipses of the sun to their failures to make the proper sacrifices that would sustain the weary sun god as he made his rounds in the sky.

For thousands of years it was customary to explain the unpleasant and painful by reference to the inscrutable workings of the deity.

Leavetaking is painful. When it happens, we seek its significance. Some of the ways in which we do this can make the situation worse.

Donald Flint is fired after fourteen years with the company. His first reaction is a mixture of rage and shock. Soon fear becomes a predominant element in the mixture. He wonders what will happen to him, whether he can get another job, how he and his family will survive.

But along with these reactions comes another. Flint looks for the meaning of the event—"Why did it happen?" At first Flint blames the stupidity of the management, the gutlessness of his boss, and the machinations of rivals. But he can't make that proposition stick. Donald Flint is convinced that, particularly in business, the merit system is all-pervasive. If you have it, you make it; if you don't have it, you fail. Failure is your own fault. So as he works to impose meaning on the event, he is driven toward blaming himself. He didn't work as hard as he might have worked. He said things he shouldn't have said. He made mistakes. Guilt becomes the dominant thread in the tapestry of significance his mind is weaving for him. He sinks into indolence and severe depression.

Another case. After eighteen years of marriage Barbara Schaefer is losing her husband. He announces that he is in love with his secretary. The secretary is getting a divorce; Schaefer wants one too. It's the answer, he says.

Barbara is dumbfounded. She has always been "a good wife." She has worked hard to make a good home for Pete and the kids. She has never been like some women in their suburban community, going out and working and neglecting the home. She has never played around, never done anything that appeared to clash with her idea of what a good wife should be.

Her friends tell her that Pete is a heartless bum, not worth caring about—"good riddance." At the same time they don't hide their surprise that Barbara "could not see this coming" from Pete's lengthening absences from home, his vague overnight trips, his remoteness and irritability when he was around the house.

Barbara is advised that the meaning of the event is simple: it is all Pete's fault. But she can't buy that. Her search for significance takes an inward turn. She has never been one to shirk responsibility, nor can she accept the idea that awful things like this "just happen." So she becomes convinced that somewhere along the line she went wrong. She was too placid; too unadventurous; not exciting enough in bed; not sparkling enough in conversation; not smart enough. Barbara Schaefer finds the meaning in this traumatic leavetaking by blaming it on herself.

By making too strenuous and too early a search for the meaning of leavetaking we may do ourselves considerable harm. The "meaning" we find is frequently embodied in a scapegoat. All too often we locate the scapegoat within ourselves.

It is no longer fashionable to attribute pain and hardship to the functioning of an all-powerful but essentially benign god whose purposes we can only dimly discern. The modern feeling is that we are indeed masters of our own fate. We "make our own breaks"; if the breaks are bad, we find the reasons in some lack in ourselves.

The tendency for self-scapegoating is especially active immediately after a severe leavetaking. We ask, "Why did this happen to me?" There is no ready answer. Our "intolerance of unintelligible events" does not permit us to settle for that. We insist on an answer. We need a frame of reference. To say it's God's will has become a cop-out. We look for others to blame (and, unjust as it may be, blaming others is healthier than blaming ourselves). Often we do not find adequate scapegoats outside ourselves. So we shoulder the blame, thus taking on another heavy burden at a time when we are least able to support it.

The mature handling of leavetaking requires that we *delay* the search for meaning until we are prepared to cope with it. It is not possible for human beings to forego altogether the need for an answer. Lack of meaning is a vacuum; the psyche rushes to fill it. But if we can, at least temporarily, fill the vacuum in some other way, we will be better prepared to come up with a positive and helpful answer when the time comes to do so.

One reason for this is that if you are able to hold off for a time in imposing meaning on a traumatic event, one part of your psyche is working in your favor. Our bodies operate to maintain homeostasis, or balance. This is exemplified by the activity of the white corpuscles, which rush to neutralize unbalancing elements in the blood. The mind, too, works to preserve homeostasis.

Leavetaking occurs. We ask, "What does it mean?" If we come up with an answer too quickly, that answer will be wrong and self-destructive. The healing processes of the psyche can help you to get through the crisis and resume the normal course of growth and life. You short-circuit those processes by locking yourself into a premature and self-accusatory certainty of the significance of the event.

We are impelled toward premature conclusions because we find it hard to accept the irretrievable loss of the familiar. When we come up with a hasty answer to the question "Why?" we run the risk of petrifying ourselves in misery. We become like the Greek women, always in mourning. We no longer mourn the loss, we mourn ourselves and our own inadequacies. Or we develop certain kinds of neurotic symptoms—phobias, compulsions, aberrant behavior. We punish ourselves for causing the leavetaking.

When bereavement comes, postpone a search for its meaning. For one thing, when you are thinking normally you know that it is impossible to grasp the meaning of everything, and equally impossible to grasp *all* of the meanings of anything.

Give yourself up to the work of mourning mindlessly, not analytically. Don't think—grieve. Let yourself go. It may be very painful to let your mind show a series of flashbacks of happier times (real or imagined), but that is better than blaming yourself for what happened.

Understand that you will be driven to look for meaning. You can't shut your mind to it, but don't give in to it either. Resist the temptation to accept hand-me-downs, other people's reasons for the happening. ("My mother walked out on my father because he was a self-centered slob; I must be the same.")

To the extent that you brood about questions, couch them in terms of courses of action rather than basic causes. Don't ask:

> Why did this happen to me?
> What have I done to deserve this?
> Where did I go wrong?

Instead, ask yourself:

> What do I do now?
> How can I get through the next couple of days?
> Where do I go from here?

Not that, in the full pain of leavetaking, you are likely to come up with workable answers to practical questions. That is not the true purpose of the questions. By concentrating on these matters of ways and means you are at least making a start on the process of growth and advancement into the next phase of your life. More important, you are withstanding the temptation to impose a "meaning" on the bereavement when that "meaning" will not only be inaccurate but self-destructive.

It is better to permit the "work of mourning" to proceed

than to look for quick answers that will make the situation worse. Left to its own devices, your psyche will begin to grow healing flesh over the lacerations. There may be scars, but function will return.

# *XVI* FALSE ALTERNATIVES

WHEN THE EMOTIONAL STORM has subsided we ask ourselves, "What do I do now?" It's a necessary progression. After leave-taking we must consider the alternatives.

Some people get sidetracked at this point. They choose alternatives, but not valid ones. They compound the difficulty and pain by setting course toward false alternatives.

The search for the false alternative can be motivated by inner confusion or outside influence. Sometimes we go down a dead-end street because we have not resolved internal conflict and determined what we really want and need. Sometimes we are impelled into a disastrous choice because of the pressure exerted by our peers or society in general. Usually the choice of the false alternative grows out of a combination of these factors.

False alternatives range from a misguided desire to build an exact duplicate of the lost relationship to an erroneous determination to do something as different as possible from what we did before. At one end of the scale is the trap of duplication; at the other end is the "landslide effect."

## The Search for Duplication

George Hannon loved the advertising-agency business.

He was very good at the peripherals. He fired off ideas at meetings. He thought about storyboards, retention scores, unique selling propositions, and all the rest of it. He was a virtuoso of the business lunch.

One problem. George Hannon was not really a very good advertising man. His copy was workable but a little clumsy. His slice-of-life campaigns were sliced too thin. His clients were never quite confident.

George was fired. He set out to find another job exactly like the one he had lost. He applied to similar agencies. They turned him down.

He received a tentative offer from a manufacturer who was looking for a reliable merchandising functionary. But this did not interest Hannon. It would mean giving up the adventurousness of agency life. He finally caught on with a small agency. It was not much of a job, but, with a stretch of the imagination, it could be made to resemble the true, exhilarating "ad game."

George Hannon is bombing out on this job as well. He is up against young tigers. They are contemptuous of his work. They snicker at his tales of how things were done at the big agency. He tries hard. These days he comes home with a headache almost every night.

Hannon is trying to *replace* a lost relationship by finding one that is closest to a facsimile of the first. He is looking for identity of details, not satisfaction of real needs. He is looking in the wrong place for what he really wants. He is in the unhappy position of the fellow in the old story who loses his wallet on Washington Street but who chooses to look for it on Main Street, two blocks away, because the light is better there.

Helen Scheffler had always felt "very close" to her older daughter, Karen. Karen was much like Helen in so many ways. They worried about the same things: efficiency in the kitchen, the right color for the drapes in the bedroom, order in the household. Helen and her daughter could spend an hour talking happily about the best ways to restore an old table.

The younger daughter, Fran, was different. At fourteen Fran had astounded her mother by reading Turgenev. Fran couldn't care less whether the drapes and bedspread matched. She had come to be reasonably neat, but that was about all.

It was not that Helen Scheffler did not love Fran as much as she did Karen. She did; but they were not friends and confidantes to anywhere near the extent to which Karen and her mother related to each other.

Karen went to college close to home. She was still around the house a lot. Helen could truly say that her elder daughter was more than a daughter; she was her best friend. Fran went to a school a thousand miles away. Her letters were warm, but she wrote about things that were not topics of everyday conversation between Helen and Karen.

When Karen began to go out seriously with a particular young man, Helen was given ample opportunity to meet him. She approved; this was the right kind of boy for Karen. But Helen Scheffler did not project the situation to its logical conclusion. Thus the engagement was something of a shock. And when Karen married and moved away—*really* moved away—Helen did not know what to do.

She tried to keep the former relationship going. There were phone calls during which mother and daughter talked about the same things they had always talked about. At first Karen initiated her share of the calls, then it seemed to be

Helen who was always doing the calling. Karen was at first loving and understanding, then she was patient. She had her own concerns. Helen realized this in a way, but she continued to try to keep up the old bond.

Karen's husband was transferred to a far-off place. Helen, sticking with it, went to visit them a couple of times. But what had once existed was not there any more. The leave-taking had happened.

For some time Helen had been turning more to Fran. She determined that she would now "get to know" her younger daughter better. Helen's way of getting to know Fran was to work doggedly at interesting Fran in the same things that had interested Karen. Helen would find a new recipe and launch into an animated discussion of it. Fran would sit for a while listening, and then make some excuse to be elsewhere.

Helen Scheffler felt increasingly disappointed and frustrated. She blamed Fran for not being as loving as Karen. Fran was a "cold fish." Why couldn't she be more responsive? After all Helen and Fran's father had done for the girl, you would think, etc., etc.

Fran moved away abruptly, and Helen was bereft. Her husband urged her to interest herself in other things. But there weren't any other things that appealed to Helen. She wanted her daughter and best friend back. Her life deteriorated into a longing for Karen.

Helen Scheffler had tried to find a substitute. She had staked her hopes on establishing a new relationship identical with the old one. To do this she had turned to the first logical candidate. After all, Fran was her daughter and Karen's sister. The fact that Fran had always acted "different" could be changed. All it took, Helen had thought, was patience and effort to "bring out" in Fran the same wonderful qualities that had made Karen such a marvelous girl. True, Karen had betrayed her mother in a way. But Helen did not blame Karen nearly as much as she blamed Fran for not being what she could have been if only she had tried. The search for a facsimile of the lost object is almost always a doomed and anguishing experience. It goes on all the time. Leave-lorn people haunt singles bars looking for a person identical to the one who went away. Job seekers struggle to find something as close as possible to the job that did not work out. Uprooted people search for the elements in the new community which are the same as those in the place that was left behind. Failing in the search, they are miserable.

## The Landslide Effect

Linda Corbin was the happiest homemaker on her block. Her children—three of them, the oldest twelve—were always smartly turned out, well fed, on time for school, warm and close to their mother. Linda was a superb cook. She searched out exotic recipes, but she did not stop there; her own concoctions were nearly always great successes. Other women held her in awe.

The Corbin house was a beautiful place, not in a cold, museumlike fashion but as a pleasant, comfortable home, ideal for living in. Linda was undoubtedly artistic; she applied her gifts to the enhancement of the living values in her home.

Moreover, she was highly organized. You could always count on her to be on time, well prepared, and fully participative. This was true of her PTA work, her efforts in behalf of the local historical society, her labors for the Welcome Wagon, and her housekeeping.

When Jeff Corbin left Linda, he went—as often happens —to the other extreme. The woman he had fallen in love with was about as undomestic as you could imagine. Her own marriage had broken up, and she was perfectly willing to let her ex-husband have the children. She was ambitious, career-oriented, hard in all the ways that Linda Corbin seemed soft.

Linda was devastated. What had she not done to create a good home and fine family life for Jeff? Now he was leaving her for a type of woman whom Linda had not disliked but for whom she felt sorry.

Thank God, Jeff had done well. There was plenty of money for Linda and the children. Jeff had managed the leavetaking so that Linda would be well taken care of. He consoled himself that Linda would marry again before too long. She was a perfect wife ("for a lot of guys, but not for me").

Indeed, there was a likely candidate right at hand. Frank Monahan was three years older than Linda. The Monahans and the Corbins had been close friends. It had been a great shock when Frank's wife died suddenly, leaving him with one young child. Frank Monahan had been a tower of strength during the Corbins' breakup. Now that Linda was available, Frank felt his affection turning into more than affection. He contemplated the idea of marrying Linda and found it in all ways a good idea.

Frank's interest was not lost on Linda. When she was being objective she had to admit that Frank would be in many ways a far better husband than Jeff had ever been. Frank was interested in doing imaginative things around the house. Jeff could not have cared less. Frank was good with children, really seemed to enjoy being around them, talking with them, doing things with them. Jeff had been dutiful, but the role of father had not exhilarated him. Linda felt at ease with Frank, liked spending time with him, and found him attractive.

Given all of these factors, one might have thought it inevitable that Linda would see more and more of Frank and that, after a suitable period, they would marry. Many friends expected this to happen. They felt their expectations were being confirmed as Frank and Linda began to show up together at social events. They were starting to be thought of as a couple.

So what was the problem? It began when one female friend of Linda's, married—but far from idyllically—said, "I envy you. It's the best break a girl could get. He's gone, and good riddance. You got a decent settlement out of him, no more than the rat owes you, and now you can get off this 'Sally-sit-by-the-fire' kick and get out into the real world."

The "real world" meant going to work at a full-time job. Linda dismissed the notion. She knew more and more women were getting jobs—many of her friends were working—but she did not figure that this was for her. She had not held a job at all except for a couple of summer vacations. All of her talent had gone into being a wife and mother. For the time being she was a mother and not a wife, but there was still plenty for her to do.

However, the refrain was taken up by other friends. What Linda needed, they agreed, was to get out into the world in a full-time occupation. Women no longer have to be chained to the role designated for them by a male-dominated world. The message that Linda was getting was that there was a whole other existence waiting for her, exciting and satisfying in ways that her previous way of living had never been. The fact that she did not feel the need to do this showed only that she had been thoroughly brainwashed.

Linda Corbin was an intelligent woman but not a strong-minded one. She always listened to people who seemed to have her best interests at heart. At first she participated pleasantly in conversations designed to get her to change direction, but she did not take them seriously. After a while, though, Linda started to wonder. Everybody was saying that she ought to get a job; maybe there was something to it. But what was the right thing for a conscientious person to do?

Linda Corbin did not particularly need the money; others needed it more. Wouldn't it really be a bad thing to take a job that someone else really needed?

Linda's friends declared that this question was not germane. That was not the way the world worked. One's most important duty was to realize to the fullest possible extent one's own personhood. It was particularly vital to women, who had been prevented from achieving true self-realization. Linda had a duty to herself, and she had a duty to the cause of women in general.

But of course there was the much more insistent problem of the children. How can I, asked Linda, go out and let them shift for themselves? It would be irresponsible. Ah, said her friends, you are saying that only because you have been so thoroughly indoctrinated with the perfidious conventional wisdom of a male chauvinist society. That kind of thinking was old-fashioned. Children *should* be on their own to a much larger extent than Linda was permitting hers to be. Only in this way could they adjust to life. Furthermore, kids were assisted in gaining emotional health by having a mother who was a fully developed human being. Sure, they *seemed* happy, well behaved, acclimated to school, and all the rest of it, but actually Linda was smothering them with mothering. They should be encouraged to be more resourceful and to mature in their own ways. And, ever and anon, there was the point that, as much as she loved the kids, Linda's greatest duty was to herself.

All this began to have its effect. Linda Corbin's attitude began to change. She no longer asked, "Why should I do it?" or "Wouldn't I be shirking my responsibilities if I do it?" Now she was beginning to wonder, But *how* can I do it?

"I'm not trained for any kind of job," Linda told a friend one day. Rightly recognizing that Linda had progressed a considerable distance along the prescribed route, her friend said, "Nonsense. You are the best-organized person I know.

Anything you want to accomplish, you accomplish. You just haven't wanted to accomplish the right things. Not trained? Baloney! You have an artistic gift and the ability to use it for very practical things. You're a smart girl—you can talk, and you get along beautifully with people. We've all been screwed long enough by being told we're not qualified. If you are willing, you can get a job you'll get real kicks out of and that will open up bigger things for you. Sure, you'll have to start small, but with what you've got on the ball, it won't be long before you're doing fine."

At last Linda Corbin gave in. One of her energetic working friends helped her get a job. It sure is starting small, Linda reflected—sales clerk in a posh art and antique shop. But, she told herself, maybe I'm being snobbish. Besides, her friend had confided that the owner of the store wanted to be able to get out of the day-to-day running of the business. When Linda's aptitudes proved out, as they no doubt would, it would not be long before she was managing the place.

With great hesitation and enormous fussiness, Linda made arrangements for the children. Fearfully she told the kids about what she was going to do. They did not dissolve in tears; they seemed to think it a curious matter, rather than evidence of lack of love or a threat to their well-being.

At first the work was difficult. Linda was good at talking with people, but she had never talked with people in any such situation. Sometimes customers could be vague to the point of utter frustration. Some shoppers were discourteous, a few even cruel.

But as Linda learned the ropes and gained some confidence in her knowledge and judgment, she found that she could handle the job all right. She began to size up her customers. Some she could guide subtly; others needed authoritative suggestions; still others required patience and a lot of listening. Linda learned more about the way a shop was managed.

She talked with suppliers; she looked at similar stores; she got ideas and voiced them.

Gradually, as predicted, Linda Corbin took over more of the running of the shop. She was doing all right; her buying sense, undeveloped at first, was shrewd. She could evaluate applicants for clerks' jobs, and she could supervise without creating an unpleasant atmosphere.

She became an accomplished store manager in a short time. She was making good money, part of it in a percentage arrangement offered by the owner. Linda Corbin had a career. It was time- and energy-consuming, of course; there were evenings when she was just too tired to be anything but perfunctory with the kids. Linda wrote it off as part of the price that one has to pay for self-fulfillment. All of her friends were impressed with what she had been able to do. Some were more than impressed; there was an edge of envy now.

One thing that diminished was attention from Frank Monahan. Linda Corbin the perfect homemaker he had seemed very interested in; Linda Corbin the brisk store manager and career woman he appeared to be less absorbed with. Their dates declined in intensity and frequency. Finally it became evident that Monahan was spending more time with another woman, one who lacked many of Linda's personal skills and attractions but who was not embarked on a career and who did not seem in any way likely to embark on one.

Linda regretted this. She found that Frank had come to mean a lot to her and that the idea of marriage to him had taken fairly firm shape in one part of her mind. But what did she care? Her career was giving her opportunities to do things and use talents in a way that had been unimaginable before.

The children certainly were more on their own—and they acted that way. They didn't show a desire to talk to their mother as often or as openly as they once had, even when the rare opportunity presented itself. This development, too, bothered Linda, but, as her friends said, the anxiety was a natural vestige of a past situation she was well out of.

Linda Corbin is still managing the shop. She has been taken into partnership, and she and her partner are thinking of opening a similar place in a nearby town. If that works, they envision a string of stores.

Linda has it made. But why does she get those agonizing headaches? Maybe it's because she is having trouble sleeping. She has to travel a lot now, and she finds this debilitating. More aspects of the work annoy her these days. She is attuned to even the most minute problem and she drives herself until it is solved.

She is not as pleasant as she used to be. There's a hardness there; she can be sharp and cutting. But all this is part of the self-fulfillment she elected to seek.

The trouble with this self-fulfillment, Linda admits, is that it makes you so damned unhappy so often. She is free. Once the notion of casual sex was alien to her. Now from time to time Linda will sleep with a man—nothing very serious, and she does not get much out of it. But even though this kind of sex is not very satisfactory, she finds herself involved in it more frequently as time goes on.

Time *does* go on; Linda is getting older, and she is conscious of this. She is also not getting any happier. She has about decided to go into therapy when her work load lightens a little. Her friends tell her that this is the right thing to do.

What Linda Corbin experienced was the "landslide effect" which goes with certain kinds of leavetaking. It is a shock. There are other important and satisfying relationships still in force, but the individual turns away from these. They are identified with the one relationship that has been broken. The person concludes that the break that has occurred should signal a complete rejection of all previous relationships, whatever their importance or state of repair.

Leavetaking—particularly abrupt involuntary leavetaking—should trigger self-analysis that holds up to examination the web of associations composing the present state of existence. The key here is *examination,* not automatic rejection. The fact that an important bond is severed does not mean that all bonds should be severed. But this is what happens. The breaking of the first relationship constitutes the tumbling rock that begins to dislodge other rocks and turns eventually into a landslide that carries the person beyond the bounds of *all* previous associations, the good ones as well as the bad ones. The result is a state of life that is undeniably different but not necessarily better.

The landslide effect is prevalent today. Moderation seems to have gone out of style. We are not really living unless we locate ourselves at the extreme end of some spectrum or other.

A complete break with all the values and associations of the past is good *for some individuals.* But, sadly, a lot of people do not make this complete break as individuals. They do it because others have done it, because others urge them to do it, because it has become the "in" thing to do.

The example of Linda Corbin is a case in point. She was not a born career woman. Jeff's pulling out was a terrible shock; he was a key part of her existence. But Jeff was not the linchpin of her whole life. Many women find that a marital leavetaking is, after the anguish dissipates, a useful watershed. They are able to break off associations that have become burdensome rather than satisfying. They now move, relatively unencumbered, into a new and more fruitful way of life that enables them to realize themselves fully.

However, what is good for some women, even a preponderance of women, is not good for all individuals. Linda Corbin's bonds to her home and her children were strong and satisfying. She was good at what she was doing and she derived positive benefit from it. In her case the best management of the leavetaking would have involved maximum conservation of those aspects of former life that were satisfying—and would continue to be satisfying—for her and for the children.

It is quite true that studies have shown that children are happier and better adjusted with one parent—a working mother, for example—than with two parents who are squabbling much of the time. However, to state the proposition that children invariably do well when they stay with a mother who goes out to work is to stretch it far beyond its real significance. Growing up in a situation in which there is only a mother whose time and energy are highly limited is *not* good for children. It is better than nothing; it is better than spending the formative years in a poisoned atmosphere. But while the need for a mother to fulfill herself is important, it does not mean a close, loving mother-child relationship has been superseded.

Linda Corbin's children are likely in the long run to be victims, not beneficiaries. Their current state of existence is piling up a debt of negative attitudes toward leavetaking which they will be called upon to pay in the future.

And, into the bargain, Linda herself is not happy with the turn her life has taken. She made a total break with the past because she was led to believe that it was the thing to do. She did not respond to her individual needs.

False alternatives can look as valid and lure as seductively as true ones. We can avoid them by gauging our vulnerability to the shocks of leavetaking and choosing effective strategies for determining the best course to follow.

THE MECHANISM THAT
HELPS YOUR WOUNDS
TO HEAL

YOUR DEFENSE MECHANISMS help to get you through a bad leavetaking. However, when some of their manifestations surface, you may not like them.

When Jeff Kimball took over as head of the department, he named young Gene Stein as second-in-command. Kimball had recognized Stein's intelligence and flair ten minutes after the younger man walked into his office to apply for a job. Kimball insisted, against the inclinations of the president and the board members, upon moving Stein up when he moved up. Kimball confided in Stein, supported him against more senior members of the department who were disgruntled by the neophyte's quick ascension, treated him like the heir apparent. One day, Kimball told himself and Stein, the two of them would be running the whole show.

So the day that Gene Stein quit was a rough day for both

of them. Stein's distress was apparent. He was close to tears as he told Kimball about the big offer from the other company. "I tried," said Stein, "but I can't really turn them down. I have kids and expenses and a career to think about. It just wouldn't be fair, not only to me but to Diane and the children. So I hope you understand, Jeff. I've got to move on. And I hope we still can be friends."

Jeff Kimball was shocked. At first he couldn't believe it. He wondered what he would do without Stein, on whom he had come to rely so heavily. He tried to talk Stein out of it; offered more money, stock, deferred compensation, a more awesome title. Gene Stein was embarrassed and uncomfortable. He insisted on taking the new job.

Finally Kimball accepted it—at least on the surface. He regained his cool. He wished Gene Stein well, told him he was doing the right thing. After Stein moved over to the other company, the two had lunch once a week—for a while. Then Kimball began to find that he was often too busy to meet Stein. The intervals stretched out—two weeks, a month. At last they were not in touch with each other at all. Kimball kept up with Stein's progress (and it was good progress) through the trade press and the business pages. About a year after the departure Kimball was talking with Carl Bell, the dependable but unspectacular performer whom he had promoted to Stein's job. Bell, commenting on a new project, said, "I came across this file of Gene Stein's outline for the structure. There are some pretty good ideas here."

Kimball shook his head. "Forget it. Stein's ideas looked okay on paper, but when you tried to run with them they were nothing. The guy was all footwork and no punch. A flash in the pan. He was lucky he left when he did. I was clouding up to get rid of him. And he'll turn out to be a flash in the pan over there too."

Fred Pohl had made it with several girls, but his relationship with Ginny was the first long-standing one. For one thing, they hadn't gone to bed right away. Ginny held back. Fred kidded her about being old-fashioned. It wasn't as if she were a virgin—she never made a thing of that—but she just could not see jumping right into the sack.

But they liked each other, and the sex came naturally. They were close. There was talk of marriage now and then, but neither one of them went very far with it. Nobody they knew was getting married. They had it good just as it was, why go through an archaic ceremony that, as each of them had seen at home, led to more trouble than pleasure?

Besides, the arrangement gave Fred a measure of freedom which he welcomed. At first he valued it merely theoretically. Then he began to put it to practical use. He got around more; he met some new people, particularly women. He went to bed with some of them—with one in particular, Lois, more than once.

Lois was different from Ginny—cooler, funnier, more unpredictable. Ginny did not much like Lois, or like Fred's seeing her. Fred never said he had gone to bed with Lois, but he never said he hadn't, either. The subject did not come up directly. But Fred could see that Ginny would like to bring it up. This bothered him. Ginny had no hold on him. He was a free person. Ginny had no right to mope about anything he did. As time went on, Ginny seemed less fun, Lois seemed more fun.

Fred thought he could just phase out with Ginny, but it was not that easy. There *was* a scene, tears, pleading, the whole bit. Fred was glad to have it over with. He still liked Ginny, she was a marvelous person in many ways, but when something was finished, it was finished. Not that he was getting into anything as deeply with Lois. For one thing, Lois didn't operate that way. But he was free.

Aftr the break there were phone calls from Ginny. Fred met her a few times for lunch. They chatted calmly; they were civilized. Fred realized again what a valuable human being Ginny was. He was sorry that the girl was so hung up on him. It was painful to know that Ginny was suffering, but that was no reason to blow his whole life.

Ginny stopped calling. Now and then Fred would see her. After a while she seemed to be always with a particular man —older, louder, not at all the kind of guy he would have thought Ginny would like. Fred thought, Rebound; she's working it out the best way she can. He felt bad. He felt even worse when he heard that Ginny and this man—married, separated, and Ginny's boss—were sleeping together quite steadily.

Fred resolved that he had been a heel. While there was no way he was going to get back into the clinging-vine thing with Ginny, he had been a little rough on her. He would see her again on a limited basis. There was nothing much to keep him from it; the deal with Lois seemed to have about petered out.

Fred called Ginny. They had lunch. He suggested dinner. Ginny was as pleasant as she could be. She said no. Fred called a week later, asked about a drink. Ginny was busy. They met at a party; Ginny was alone. Fred positioned himself to ditch the woman he had come with, and at what he took to be the right moment, he mentioned to Ginny that they might go on to someplace else. Ginny left by herself.

This went on sporadically for another month. Finally Ginny said, "Look, Fred. You're dear to me. I think we had a great time together. It's over now. I have something else, and somebody else." Fred was perplexed, then infuriated.

Nowadays Fred is a fount of anecdotes about Ginny. He is informative about her shortcomings in bed and out. He is, as he sees it, caustically witty about Ginny's desperation and her dumbness in settling for a no-win affair with an old slob. He can recite a catalog of Ginny's unpleasant habits and juvenile hangups. Fred's friends are beginning to get very bored with it all.

When Althea Moon learned that her husband was being transferred to San Diego she was shocked and unhappy. They had lived in the environs of Boston for nine years. They had friends; in particular, Moon had her own circle of friends and her own routine of activities. She did community work, which she liked and which brought her into contact with people who were congenial. She knew how to *enjoy* life in that location and had never thought about moving any place else.

But Althea Moon's husband had compelling arguments. The youngest of their children was about to graduate from high school, so there could no longer be any question of uprooting the kids from a school situation. Besides, their older daughter was at UCLA, and their graduating son was leaning toward a West Coast college, so they would be much closer. And then there was the weather. Althea Moon had never handled the winters too well, and it seemed to get worse as time went on. Here at least was a chance for living in the perpetual sun. Moreover, Althea was told—as all initially reluctant émigrés to southern California are told—that within a one-hour drive one may find anything he wants: snow, desert, woods, skiing, swimming, swinging, gambling. After a while Moon began to get used to the idea.

The big thing was the new job. Althea Moon's husband would be making a lot more money than he had made before. He would have prestige and power to a degree that had been denied him heretofore. And while Althea had rather gotten out of the habit of thinking that those things shed reflected glory on her and enriched her life, she managed to regain a useful portion of such a frame of mind.

Nevertheless it was tough for Moon to say goodbye to her friends and colleagues. It was not just the severing of pleasant relationships. Althea Moon had become a mainstay of some community organizations. Now she would have to leave pet projects in the hands of others, pull out of responsibilities that needed to be undertaken and that she thought, frankly, she could handle better than anyone else.

The move went off smoothly. The house in La Jolla was magnificent. Mr. Moon was ushered into his new post with a gratifying show of respect. Althea Moon found a new and variegated world of things to see and do.

She still had the urge to work in worthwhile community enterprises. This did not work out so well. Local circles were hard to break into. There were, of course, low-level jobs she could do, but the decision-making spots were occupied, and Moon was used to holding some. Her friends back east had been people with whom she could talk earnestly about betterment and beautification. On the Coast their friends were all connected with her husband's work. They were nice people, but they did not think or talk in the ways that she was accustomed to.

But money and freedom to do what you like can fill in lots of gaps. Althea Moon adjusted. She regrouped into the configuration of the powerful big shot's wife. The community could take care of itself. Others would slave away at their often thankless labors; Althea Moon would now enjoy. This she proceeded to do.

Ten months later Althea had occasion to go back to Boston for a couple of days on a trip with her husband. She looked up some old acquaintances. They got together for a pleasant reunion. The first jarring note for the old acquaintances came when Althea greeted the mention of a once-cherished project with a merry laugh: "Are you girls still wasting your time on that junk? Nothing will ever come of it anyway. You do this kind of thing and people just think you're a bunch of crazy old biddies!"

There was much more in this vein. The old friends, who considered themselves—and certainly their public image—to be anything but that of a bunch of crazy old biddies, smiled and tried to change the subject. No matter whatever subject might be chosen, Althea was ready to heap casual scorn on public-spirited earnestness and extol the joys of just enjoying life. "But of course you have to be able to afford it."

There was nothing about her former milieu or neighborhood that seemed now to amount to anything but a joke to Althea. She had funny and caustic things to say about the weather, the stodginess of the people, the backwardness of the culture and the unstimulating nature of the whole environment. After what seemed an eternity to the old acquaintances the reunion broke up. They would never see Althea Moon again, and that was all right with them. As for Althea, she was glad she had had a chance to see what she had left and to remind herself of how little she was losing by leaving it.

These people—Althea, Fred, Kimball—are suffering from something known as "cognitive dissonance," induced by leavetaking. They are reducing the dissonance, but in a negative way.

The psychologist Leon Festinger introduced the concept of cognitive dissonance. The essence of Festinger's proposition is that circumstances—difficult decisions, for example, or such distressing episodes as severe leavetaking—create a dissonance in the psyche. The mind works to resolve the dissonance. The means of resolution may take various forms. The resolution may be brief or protracted. Our conscious minds usually are not aware of what is going on.

Here is one way that experimenters have tested the theory. A group of high school students are asked to rate ten popular records in order of preference. Then the students are told that they will be given, free, three of the records. However, the gifts do not consist of their top choices. Instead, a teenager may be given her second, fifth and eighth selections. Some time later the kids are asked again to rate the same list of records. The records that they received as gifts come out much higher than before, frequently one-two-three.

Psychologists describe what has happened this way: a dissonance was set up by the discrepancy between objective preference and actual possession of less-desired objects—between idealized image and actual fact. The psyche has worked to make actual fact more acceptable. It has switched conscious opinion over to the posture of deciding that what has really happened is the best thing that could have happened. The adage that a bird in the hand is worth two in the bush becomes true in the sense that the mind comes around to the notion that the bird in the hand *is* better, whatever might have been thought before.

Members of the advertising and marketing profession are familiar with this phenomenon, though they may not call it cognitive dissonance. Advertising research departments note that people who have made a large purchase—a car, say—may spend more time looking at the commercials for that particular car than they did before they made the buy. There is no practical sense to it; the die has been cast. But the psyche needs reassurance that the right thing has happened. Otherwise the dissonance will persist. When you see people in the library looking things up in *Consumer Reports,* they are often reading about items they have already bought. Their minds are not in harmony about the decision; they need to resolve the discord. Skillful salesmen spend time with customers after the sale has been made. "Post-selling," they call it; it is a way of reducing cognitive dissonance.

We don't understand in detail how the mind operates to reduce dissonance, but we know that it does so. On the whole, the phenomenon is a healthy one. We are protected from hurt. The process may cause some conscious distress, as do the distress-fighting mechanisms of the body when their efforts push temperatures higher than normal.

But there is a major problem with the way in which we may resolve our cognitive dissonances. The resolution can be positive. It may also be negative.

The youngsters in the experiment with the popular records resolve the conflict, by and large, in a positive way. They rate the gift records higher than they did before, bestowing more esteem on the records and on themselves for being the possessors of them. However, let's assume a student, asked for the second set of rankings, places his gifts at the bottom of the list. In effect he is saying that anything he has received this easily is no good. He is denigrating the gift and himself. He is saying that nothing good happens to him. The dissonance is resolved, but in a negative way. The price may be high.

Leavetaking seems to be particularly conducive to negative resolution of dissonance. One common means by which the mind restores psychic harmony is by attack on the merit of the person or situation from which we have been parted. The virulence of the attack is apt to increase to the degree that the lost object is valuable to us. The boss who has lost an esteemed subordinate can be heard a year later expounding on the uselessness and even the moral deficiency of that same subordinate. The person who has felt a sense of loss in leaving a home and friends of long standing seems heartlessly callous in criticizing what has been left behind. The abandoned lover engages in hateful gossip about the person who was once loved.

When this happens, psychic balance is being restored, but the side effects are emphatically unpleasant. We hurt other people when we denigrate what we have said goodbye to. Furthermore, the act of denigration, while it seems to reduce inner tension and no doubt works toward the long-range reestablishment of psychic harmony, does not really make us feel better. On one level the boss knows that he is being unfair to his former subordinate, and the forsaken lover knows he is being unjustly spiteful about his one-time partner. True, on another level the leavetaken individual believes those things when he says them. He will, however, continue to receive guilty flashes of awareness that what he is doing is wrong.

Scapegoating is another means of resolution. A culprit must be found to bear the blame for the unhappiness. So some innocent bystander is chosen, and the result is injustice to the scapegoat and unhappiness for the assigner of the blame. Our loved ones often become scapegoats for our frustrations.

These are the traps into which we can be led by negative resolution of dissonance. We heap scorn and belittlement on the people, places and things that we have taken leave of. (And, incidentally, we may do this whether we took the initiative in the leavetaking or not.) We hunt for guilty parties on whom to place the blame. And through it all we demean ourselves and make ourselves miserable. We say, in effect, that because we are unworthy, we cannot expect anything better to happen to us.

There is no way to control or circumvent unconscious processes. The psyche will go about its work of resolving dissonances whether we wish it to or not. It is, after all, performing a survival-oriented function.

But we can be aware of the mechanism. We can remember that the process is going forward, and we can be on guard against the negative turns that it may take. When we find ourselves turning against old friends and acquaintances, or focusing vindictively on someone as the source of our trouble, we should be warned that the harmony-inducing impulses of the unconscious are beginning to work in ways that we will not like.

At this point, while it is not possible to abort or reverse the process, we can turn to certain offsetting modes of thought and behavior that will assure that the work of healing continues but that its manifestations do not hurt us or other people needlessly.

# *XVIII* GAUGING YOUR VULNERABILITY

To STRENGTHEN OUR DEFENSES against the most destructive effects of leavetaking we must know where we are vulnerable. Since the degree of vulnerability has been influenced greatly by what happened when we were children, it's worth while to begin with early experiences.

You can't be objective. We look back on childhood through a glass distorted by subjective emotions and the tricks of memory. But for the purpose of forming an idea of your present attitude toward leavetaking, it is not necessary to remember what actually happened. The important thing is how you feel *now* about the experiences of that period of life.

Start with the time before you entered school:

    1. Were most of your friends older than you?

    2. Did you stay home a great deal, going out to play infrequently?

3. Did you feel that your mother deserted you when you needed her?
4. Were you left for long periods—say three weeks—in the care of strangers?
5. Were you ever frightened by a stranger?
6. Did you have trouble finding things to do when you were alone; were you just waiting for your mother to come back?
7. Did you wait for other children to make friends with you rather than approach them?

Then you went to school:

8. Was your first day in school anxious or frightening?
9. Did you resist returning to school after the first few days?
10. Did you feel that a special friend told someone else a secret that you had both sworn never to tell?
11. Did you feel rejected by a group of children in your neighborhood?
12. Were you very fearful when you got lost?
13. Did you hurry home as soon as the final school bell rang?
14. On your first night away from home, were you frightened enough to want your mother to come and get you?
15. If you went to camp, did you dislike the experience and long for the day you could return home?

When children reach their teens they usually form relationships outside the home:

16. As you entered the teens, did you feel relatively bereft of friends?
17. Did you feel that there were groups that did not accept you?
18. When you lost friends, were they hard to replace?
19. Did you worry often that your parents might die?

20. When someone you liked died or moved away, were you depressed for a long time?
21. Did you seek emotionally involved relationships with the opposite sex?
22. If you served in the military, were you so lonely that you could not function effectively?
23. In the service (or when away from home) did you tend to seek friends from your old neighborhood or of similar religion or background?

Now a look at yourself today:

24. Have you had the same friends for a long time without acquiring new friends?
25. When a friendship ends are you unhappy for a long time?
26. Do you hold back from confiding in your friends because you fear they will violate your confidences?
27. When you have parted from a friend, has it usually been on the friend's initiative?
28. If it were possible, would you resume an old friendship—even if it was the other person who terminated it originally?
29. Do you feel anxious if you are forced to eat alone?
30. Do you think often about death?
31. Is it difficult for you to say goodbye at a party, and are you usually among the last to leave?
32. Have you stopped exploring new interests—hobbies, organizations, sports?

Now let's look at your feelings about your children.

33. Are you troubled when your children prefer to spend time with others rather than with you?
34. When children go away, do you worry constantly about something happening to them even though you know they are in good hands?
35. Do you pride yourself on your child's dependency

on you and feel good when children come to you
with minor problems?

36. If your parents were very protective of you, do you
try to treat your children in the same fashion?

As you get older . . .

37. Do you worry about the loss of youth and vigor?

38. When you get tired more quickly than you used to,
do you become depressed?

39. Do you buy clothes or adopt hair styles that accentuate youthfulness?

40. Do you automatically reject new music or new art
forms rather than try to understand them?

41. Have you turned down a job opportunity because it
involved new challenges or a move to a different
place?

42. Do you feel that the time is never quite right to go
back to school, learn new things?

Most of us would answer "yes" to about half of these
questions. If you answered "no" to most of them—say thirty
or more of the forty-two—you are relatively secure against
serious leavetaking problems.

If, however, you answered "yes" to most of the questions,
you are likely to be vulnerable to leavetaking problems.

What if, after real effort, you are unable to remember
enough about your earlier life to be able to answer at all?
Such extensive blocking of the past may indicate psychological
difficulties of some seriousness. It is reasonable to say that
inability to remember is apt to mean that you are prone to
leavetaking problems.

There is a scale of leavetaking values. At one end of the
scale is the "never take a chance" approach. The individual
who adopts this pattern never forms close relationships,
roams through life without ties, avoids the risk of pain by
staying out of situations that might involve difficult goodbyes.

At the other end of the scale is the "never let go" approach.

Here the individual seeks insatiably to form more and stronger emotional ties, fights by every possible means to maintain relationships, is always hurt when the time comes to leave. This person never takes leave voluntarily. The parting is always involuntary, always a shock, always painful.

Most of us fall somewhere in between. If you have answered "yes" to the majority of the questions, you are probably close to one or another of the extremes of the scale. The next step is to learn more about the nature of your vulnerability.

Let's say you conclude in all honesty that you do not form very strong attachments to people, places or things. In effect, you always have your psychic bags packed, ready to move on. On the surface this might appear to be a well-protected position. The most simplistic view would seem to be that if we don't form close relationships we can't get hurt by the rupture of such relationships.

But that is a deceptive view. A life lived without close relationships is a barren life. The person who lives this way is giving up far too much in the effort to avoid pain.

Furthermore, pain comes anyway. Even the most adamantly independent individual forms attachments. They sneak up on us. And leavetaking can be devastating when it happens to the individual who was not aware of any vulnerability.

There are other sources of damage for the "never take a chance" person. The man or woman who tries to adventure through life like Ulysses, avoiding closeness in all its forms, is bound to hurt other people. The adventurer will break ties in ways that make others terribly unhappy. He will withhold friendship and affection from those who need them and who are entitled to them. While the adventurer himself may appear to go unscathed for a while, he is pursuing a "scorched-earth" policy that destroys the chances for closeness when the time comes that he *does* need it. And that time comes for all of us. There is no loneliness more poignant than the loneliness of the loner, the individual who has rejected companionship and intimacy for much of his life and who now seeks them in vain.

Moreover, the "no-risk" operator cannot fully insulate himself from awareness of the pain he causes for others. With the knowledge of this pain comes guilt. It may be larded over with selfishness and assuaged with self-assurances that we live in a dog-eat-dog world and that we have to look out for ourselves. By looking out only for ourselves we ultimately betray ourselves. Below the surface the residue of guilt builds until it reaches proportions that push us into neurosis and toward psychosis. And when this happens we have no one to whom we can turn for friendship and affection.

For the person at the other end of the scale—the "never let go" person—life is a succession of dismal anticipations of being abandoned, frustrating and humiliating struggle to avoid being abandoned, and shock and hurt when the abandonment comes to pass.

Where do you stand on the scale? At which points are you most vulnerable to potential damage from leavetaking?

One way of finding out is by thinking about contingencies —"What if . . ." Begin with the most obvious possibilities. Consider the person who is closest to you. Suppose that tomorrow that person left you. You would of course feel bad. But how bad? Would you be utterly crushed? Would you go to any lengths to repair the break—promise anything, give up anything, change everything? Failing that, would you seek a replacement relationship that would be as close as possible to the one lost? Would you be extremely angry? At whom— yourself or the other person?

Suppose the person closest to you were to die? Would your grief bring despair? Would you feel guilty about all of the things you might have said or done and now will never be able to? Would you, indeed, be able to believe or accept the fact of permanent loss?

Move outward from the person closest to you. Think about

others who are close but not quite as close. Spell out for yourself, to the extent that you can, how you would feel and what you would do in the case of leavetaking from each individual. Don't skip over anybody. There are some people we take for granted; they may be neighbors, friends, working associates. We don't regard ourselves as having formed any great attachment to them, but when the bonds are broken we discover that they were much more substantial than we had thought. Look for those people in your life who are "always there." Sometimes we may be more hurt by the loss of such people than by the loss of persons whom we assume to be closer to us.

Do not restrict your contemplation of possibilities to the loss of people. There are other elements in life—places, things, situations—to which we become attached and from which leavetaking may be difficult. If you have lived in a certain place for some length of time, you may have come to take it for granted. Perhaps you feel that you don't even like it much. But you may have formed a greater attachment to location than you think. Contemplate the possibility that you might have to relocate suddenly. Think of the factors in your everyday life that are related to your present home and community. Imagine that they are removed from your existence. You may find that you would miss certain things a great deal and that the leavetaking would be a hard one.

We all work, whether we get paid for it or not. It's commonplace to focus on the less pleasant parts of work and to wish sometimes for the "big score"—the unexpected legacy, the windfall, the grand prize—that would make it possible to stop working.

Pulling out of a job—whether the job involves salaried effort, community volunteer labor, or the task of maintaining a home and raising a family—can leave a void. Work is a community to which we belong as well as a necessary occupation. Suppose that tomorrow your occupation were to end.

You would move to a different job or you would not work at all. How much would you miss it? Which parts of the routine have become embedded in your life? Who are the people you'd be sad not to see any more? What psychic fringe benefits have you come to rely on?

Another way of developing a sense of your own vulnerability is to think back on a leavetaking experience and analyze your reaction to it. Pick an experience important enough to have made a distinct impression, one that happened long enough ago so that you can consider it with a fair amount of objectivity, but not so long ago that you can't remember what really happened or how you felt.

Let's say you are remembering an involuntary leavetaking, one that came as a surprise. The normal series of reactions would be disbelief . . . shock . . . anger . . . anxiety . . . adjustment . . . acceptance . . . healing. Try to identify each of these reactions in your own thinking at the time.

Now, does any element of the series seem, in retrospect, to have been exaggerated or lacking? When the facts of leavetaking are clear, the initial denial reaction—though it may be sharp and agonizing—does not last long. Furthermore, normal and mature people do not continue to *act* in contradiction to the facts.

So when a sudden leavetaking struck you, you are likely to have been incredulous. But did you continue to disbelieve for an extended stretch of time, even when the evidence was overwhelming? More important, did you *act* as if the thing had not happened, in the face of the objective facts indicating that it had happened? When people become trapped in the denial phase, the consequences can be heavy. If you detect a tendency to act in denial of the fact of leavetaking, you have a weakness right at the initial stage of the process.

Sometimes the vulnerability comes later. An individual may pass through the first stages of the healing process normally, but the wound may never really heal properly. One way that this manifests itself is by a quixotic search for an exact replica of what has been taken away, rather than an effort to fill the void by growing into a new phase of life. A woman loses the man she loves. She ultimately accepts the fact that her former lover is gone, but she makes desperate efforts to find another man who looks and talks just like the departed mate. A middle-aged man who has always been inordinately proud of his ability as a tennis player loses a measure of speed and power on the court. Instead of accommodating himself to suitable competition, he continues to seek out younger and stronger opponents until the situation becomes embarrassing.

Some people find in analyzing their reactions to a significant leavetaking that they felt little, if anything. A teen-age boy's father dies suddenly. The boy goes through the motions of mourning, but he does not really feel as broken up as he thinks he ought to feel. Such remoteness may seem to be a kind of protection against the pain of leavetaking, but that is illusory. When we do not respond deeply to the cessation of a close relationship, we may be seeing in ourselves an inability to form any kind of attachment. This is not good. It leads to guilt, and ultimately it leads to awful loneliness.

Having thought about leavetaking situations of the past and about your reactions to them at various phases of life, you should begin to spot the areas in which you are most vulnerable. You may be overly conscious of others—or not conscious enough. You may tend to become too attached to persons and situations—or you may not be able to form attachments. You may go overboard in denying the facts, or in seeking scapegoats, or in trying to go backward in time to recreate that which does not exist any more. Self-understanding that comes from this kind of analysis is essential to your ability to handle leavetaking.

# *XIX* HOW FIELD-DEPENDENT ARE YOU?

A SOUTH AFRICAN WOMAN (white), fed up with apartheid, left her country to live in the United States. Two years later she returned to live again in Johannesburg. She knew that the situation there was, if anything, worse than before. But she had to go back. "I didn't like the grass in Arizona," she said, "or the way the flowers grow in Maine. In California the Pacific 'plopped'; I remembered how the Indian Ocean roared. These crazy external things drove me home."

Certain people are much more responsive to environment than others. Some of us are, in David Riesman's term, "gyroscope" people; some are "radar" people. "Radar" people are easily affected by their surroundings and what is happening outside them. "Gyroscope" people are attuned to signals from within.

Experiments have demonstrated the varying ways in which different individuals perceive and react to environmental change. Some researchers, for example, use the "tilted room" technique. They place people in what seems an ordinary room, and then by degrees change the configuration of the space. Some subjects feel little or nothing; others experience some mild dizziness or nausea; still others are made really sick.

Those who respond markedly to outside factors are called field-dependent. Those who do not are called field-independent. It has been found that field-independent people are better able than others to withstand the pressures of social and environmental change. They are less anxious, have a higher level of self-esteem, and think of themselves as more adequate than do those who are field-dependent.

The Rorschach test helps us to distinguish between field-dependent and field-independent individuals. When shown an inkblot the dependent personality typically responds to the color in the blot, while the independent individual sees the movement. The field-dependent person says, "I see fire and blood . . . a sunset . . . a dark, depressing cavern." His opposite will look at the same images and see "two people dancing . . . a man carrying a basket," and so on.

Your susceptibility to external cues can have considerable effects on your life. For example, why are some of us able to lose weight and stay thin, while others keep going off their diets and stay fat? A study was made of Orthodox Jews who fasted during Yom Kippur. While inside the synagogue, sitting through a day-long fast, field-independent people suffered the pangs of hunger. They suffered the same pangs when they left the synagogue. But they were able to withstand their temptations to eat to excess. These people stay thin.

The field-dependent Jews felt no symptoms of hunger during the period of fasting. They were totally involved in the ritual. Once they got outside, however, it was different. At the first scent of an Italian bakery, for instance, these persons were driven to eat frantically.

The extent to which you are dependent on the "field"—what happens around you as compared to what happens inside you—may determine the degree to which you are susceptible to leavetaking damage. This is more or less true with regard to leavetakings of a number of kinds. It is particularly true when you move from one community to another.

Field-dependent individuals are unshielded from their surroundings. They react sharply to outside situations and events. When they remain in one place for a while, with a stable set of relationships, they get used to things. Their sensitivity to the field seems to diminish. When such people are projected into new situations, however, they react vigorously—sometimes extremely—to change. The reaction is usually painful rather than pleasant.

Most of us have some problems of adjustment when we relocate. Field-dependent people have greater problems. If we are aware of our dependence, we can be better prepared for the shock.

John Hersey, observing former President Gerald Ford at work, noted that Ford tended to change his posture depending on the person to whom he was talking. When a professional type sat across the desk, Ford slumped. When a general entered, Ford straightened and squared his shoulders. Mr. Ford was a field-dependent President, and it showed in his administration and his campaign for election. President Carter may seem to be field-dependent, but he is not. He runs attuned to his inner gyroscope. It might be noted that Richard Nixon was so field-independent as to be completely removed from reality.

Field-independence is not invariably a desirable characteristic, particularly for people who need awareness of what is going on. But it can help a lot in facilitating adjustment to change.

The normal maturing process leads toward greater field-independence. Infants are completely reliant on the immediate environment. As we grow older we develop interior stabilizing mechanisms which reduce our responsiveness to external stimuli. In some adults the process is far more advanced than in others.

How field-dependent or independent are you? Here are some questions that can help you to understand your vulnerability to the effects of what goes on around you.

1. When you were a child, did you usually have other children around you?

2. On social occasions, do you prefer others to make the decisions about where to go and what to do?

3. Do you experience physical sensations or desires that are brought on by what you see? (Once a movie theater showed *Lawrence of Arabia* followed by *Scott of the Antarctic*. During *Lawrence* there was a great demand for cold drinks. When the film was about the regions of ice and snow, people bought hot coffee.)

4. Do you adjust your opinions when others express theirs? (Two people have just seen a show. One says, "I liked it." The second says, "It was lousy." The first then says, "Maybe you're right.")

5. When someone tells a joke that is not particularly funny, do you laugh readily?

6. Do you cry at such events as weddings, movies, parades?

7. When someone cuts you off in traffic, are you enraged to the extent that you keep thinking about it?

8. Do bright colors and bold designs rivet your attention?

9. When you drive through an unfamiliar neighborhood, do you notice what's around you rather than remaining fixed on getting to your destination?

10. Do you like to have people around you most of the time?

11. When you have nothing to do, is your impulse to call friends rather than read a book or watch television?
12. Do you work best in concert with others rather than alone?
13. Do you have trouble sleeping in an unfamiliar place?
14. Do you feel at a loss when there is little or no activity around you?
15. Do you form a lot of casual attachments?

If you answered "yes" to ten or more of these questions you are likely to be a field-dependent person; if your answer was "no" to ten or more, then you may be described as field-independent.

Other questions and criteria will occur to you. Childhood is, as always, a substantial factor. (The "only child" tends toward field-independence.) There is no rigidly defined boundary; it is a continuum. Some of us are more involved with what goes on around us than others. Those who are closest to either end of the continuum are more likely to have problems or to cause problems for other people. For example, the more field-dependent you are, the more susceptible you will be to social isolation.

The healthy person is neither acutely dependent on his surroundings nor altogether impervious to them. As we mature we develop the ability to filter outside influences and place them in proper perspective. Along with this, we build inner resources that offset the most damaging effects of outside events.

# XX HOW TO ASSESS A RELATIONSHIP

THE BUILDING of a strategy of leavetaking requires knowledge of the state of repair of your present relationships. Which of your associations are solid and satisfying? Which are becoming threadbare? What areas need rejuvenation? Which relationships are approaching the danger point?

Let's take inventory.

Examination of current relationships does not imply disloyalty or a wish to live without commitment. Such self-examination is, rather, a sensible measure for the preservation of psychological health. It is similar to the annual physical checkup.

In assessing our various relationships we have to know what to look for. We need to be able to separate each relationship into its principal components.

Daily life can be divided roughly into three categories of activities: personal, social, occupational. Personal living includes your inner life—the things you think about, the things you do when you are on your own. Social living is dealing with others in a nonwork context—talking with members of the family or friends, going to parties, interacting with others. Occupational time is the discharge of responsibilities—on the job, taking care of the children, maintaining the house, and so on.

The categories overlap. A person cleaning a house is also engaged in "personal" living—thinking about things. We interact with people on the job in ways that may be social as well as occupational.

Every relationship contains a number of elements that contribute to the degree of damage that may be done when the bond is broken.

One element is *time*—the number of minutes and hours per day or week that are consumed in the maintenance of the relationship. For example, a man may spend forty hours a week on the job and another ten hours working on job-connected matters that he brings home. During the week he sees his wife for, say, twelve hours, and his children for half that. On weekends—theoretically—he spends time with his family. But actually he does not see all that much of them. He plays golf, goes boating, works at his hobby. His total family time comes to considerably less than his job time.

Consider the relative effects on this man of the breaking off of his family relationship versus the loss of his job. Leavetaking from the job is not necessarily more traumatic than leavetaking from spouse and children, because there are other elements besides that of time. Nevertheless time is important. We become accustomed to certain ways of filling our waking hours. The ending of an attachment that consumed sixty hours a week leaves an enormous time gap to be filled, even if the emotional involvement with this attachment has been modest. Conversely, the cessation of a relationship that involved just a few hours a week, no matter how "close" that attachment may have seemed in terms of psychic involvement, does not leave a big time gap.

There is the matter of *tenure*—the length of time the relationship has been in effect. The longer we know a person, or remain in a situation, the more we become psychically entwined. A man may be spending fifty to sixty hours a week on his job, as against twenty hours a week with his wife. But he has held the job for just a year. He has been married for twelve years. The marital relationship has worked its way deep into his makeup. The first blush of intense emotion may have paled, but the attachment has established itself in deep psychic grooves. He devotes more time to the job, but he is not "habituated" to the job to anywhere near the same degree.

Another factor contributing to the grip of an attachment is *intensity*. A woman has been married for twenty years. She sees a great deal of her husband; they are together most evenings and weekends. She has recently become involved in community activities after having devoted herself to the task of motherhood for a long time. She faces new challenges, meets new people.

The community activity is of recent vintage. It takes up less time than family activity. But the woman has thrown herself into it with great vigor. She is living fairly intensely when she is talking with her new acquaintances and coping with her new challenges. She is fond of husband and family, but she is used to them. Her involvement with that relationship, though it is of long tenure and takes up considerable time, is less intense.

Yet another factor is what we might call the "give-take ratio" of a relationship. Every association of any importance requires us to contribute something as well as taking something away.

In the healthiest of relationships this ratio is in near balance. One individual does not contribute the same things that he gets out of it, but he gives about as much as he gets. For instance, two people live together. For one person love and sex are extremely important. The time spent immediately before, during, and after the act of sex is satisfying and glorious. Other elements of the association do not have the same grip.

The other person does not derive that much of a thrill from sex. The accouterments of romance are less important. The main benefits that this second person draws from the alliance are companionship, sympathy, social affiliation.

For each individual there is a measure of attachment and a measure of dependency. Moreover, the relationship is not unalloyed pleasure for either of them. Pleasure predominates, but it is leavened with some anxiety, some concern, some inconvenience, some pain. These are aspects of human affiliation. Furthermore, when the time for leavetaking arrives, they may be nearly as hard to give up as the purely pleasurable elements of the association.

The association may include a *situational* or "convenience" element. This factor comprises the practical considerations inherent in the affiliation. These are most readily apparent in the relationship between individual and job. A job provides money; but it provides other things as well. One's occupation establishes his status in the community. It constitutes a convenient label. When we meet new people we say, "I'm regional marketing director for Zodiac Waffles." (John Kenneth Galbraith observes: " 'Who are you with?' Until this is known, the individual is a cipher.") Industrial psychologist Harry Levinson calls this phenomenon "reciprocity"—deriving strength from being associated with a large organization. Sometimes one can draw strength by rooting for a successful athletic team.

Most relationships involve situational elements. Aside from emotional factors, marriage is a convenience and a determinant of a large part of life. In most communities, people who see each other regularly have the same marital status. A person who has been married for years becomes part of a social circle made up of other married couples. There is a separation. The individual still may be asked to the same homes for the same parties—for a while. But gradually the system closes to exclude the person, who has become "different."

People who live in intimacy with each other come to a convenient mutual sharing of the duties of life, small and large. He earns the money; she takes care of the kids. She balances the checkbook; he takes out the garbage. Such factors—easy to overlook—have a bearing on the effects of leavetaking.

Think about a relationship that is important to you. It may be a personal relationship with someone to whom you feel very close—a mate, a good friend, a child. It may involve your occupation. It may have to do with the community and circle of friends of which you have become a part. Consider the relationship in the light of the five elements we have been discussing: time involvement, tenure, intensity, give/take ratio, situational aspects.

How much of your *time* is involved in the relationship? Would its cessation open up large gaps in your routine that you would have difficulty in filling? Or, on the contrary, does the relationship seem now to take more time than you are willing to give it? Do you count on the activity called for by the affiliation or do you grudge it? If the association were to end, how would you spend your time?

What is the *tenure* of the relationship? When did it come into being? Long ago? Recently? Has it existed for so long that you've become used to it? Or is it still a fresh experience? (Thinking back to the element of time consumed by the relationship, if you are surprised at the time it takes, you may well have been involved in it for so long that it has become second nature.)

How about the *intensity* with which you pursue the involvement? Do you enjoy it? Do you take it for granted? When you are not involved in it, do you look forward to its resumption? Do the incidents of the relationship stand out vividly in your mind—or do they tend to blur? Are occasions of some time ago still fresh in your memory? Does your involvement sometimes make you feel very good—and hurt at other times? Are there considerable challenges that come with the affiliation—or is it all fairly routine?

How does your give/take ratio stand? What do you get out of the attachment? Pleasure? Stimulation? Help? Convenience? Companionship? What are you called upon to contribute? Do you feel that you give more than you get? Get more than you give? Or is it a fair exchange? Has the ratio changed? For example, do you now feel that you have to put in more and more while getting less and less out of it? In terms of what you give, do you feel your contribution is recognized and appreciated? Do you manifest appreciation for what you take? How do you do this? How much would you miss what you are getting out of the situation? To what extent would you feel compelled to continue to make the kinds of contributions you are making to this relationship in a totally different relationship? Do you need it as much as you used to? Are there needs that are not being fulfilled by any present association?

How about your *situational* involvement? To what extent does the present relationship make life easier? What large practical needs are met by it? What small details are taken care of for you? What things of a practical nature do you do for the other person or persons? How would you handle these practicalities if the association were to end? What would the other person do? Would you be in serious trouble—financially, socially—if the relationship were broken? Would you feel guilty about discontinuing your handling of the share of situational considerations?

By analyzing a current relationship in terms of these factors, you give yourself a better picture of the shape the relationship is in. You form an idea of the areas in which you would be most vulnerable if and when leavetaking comes. And you examine the association with an eye toward determining how long it is likely to last, and if, indeed, you should think about changing or discontinuing it yourself rather than having the break come about involuntarily.

Leavetaking creates emptiness. The breaking of an association will result in a void in your life; no question of that. The questions are, rather, what nature will that void take, and what must you do to fill it?

The gap may be mainly emotional. You may have built up such a psychic involvement in a person or situation that your inner life will lose focus when the association ends. This is not just a matter of how much pleasure the relationship has given you; it relates to pain as well. If your feelings relating to the affiliation are intense—plus or minus—you will need another emotional outlet.

Or the gap to be filled may be one of time. You are used to occupying yourself in a certain way. There is comfort in the routine, even though the emotional peaks and valleys may have been evened out by the erosion of time and familiarity.

The nature of the void may, however, consist principally of more practical matters—the *situational* elements. You may be quickly impelled by circumstances to find some way to fill the gap because of the exigencies of living.

Chances are that any major leavetaking combines all of these factors in the nature of the void that it creates. But certain elements will loom larger than others. Know in advance which will be the most important to you.

# XXI WHEN YOU SEE THE SIGNS THAT LEAVETAKING IS COMING

SOME LEAVETAKINGS can be foretold with a moment's thought or a glance at the calendar. We know, for example, that children who have grown will go away. Nevertheless this departure comes as a shock to many parents. They do not anticipate the event because they don't want to anticipate it. They act on the age-old defense mechanism that leads us to believe that if you ignore the imminence of something unpleasant, it won't happen. Some defense mechanisms have constructive results. This one has none at all, yet people continue to employ it.

So the first necessity in anticipating leavetaking situations is to want to anticipate them, or at least to acknowledge their inevitability and conclude that one might as well know what is going to happen rather than having it always come as a distasteful surprise. The individual who goes through life constantly surprised is a person who is destined for much un-happiness.

Shutting your eyes does not stop the world. You begin to cross the street. A car is bearing down on you. What should you do—get out of the way or pretend it is not there?

Start to take inventory of the leavetaking prospects that lie ahead. Those involving growing children are utterly predictable. Others are predictable too. If you have a job that will require you to move to another location in two years, it is common sense not to permit yourself to feel that you are settled forever.

Other partings are not quite as easily predicted as that. But leavetaking almost never happens without some warning. It is just that we allow ourselves to ignore the warning bells.

A boyfriend who used to see a girl four nights a week and call her up on the other nights now seems to be available only one night a week and almost never calls. An assistant depart-ment head who once had easy entrée to his boss's office now discovers that the boss is almost invariably in conference when he wants to drop by. A friend with whom you shared child-transporting duty on a fifty-fifty basis still calls on you for help but provides no help herself.

You can spot leavetaking behavior in others by comparative observation of three factors: time, intensity, the give/take ratio. A significant change in behavior is analogous to the warning sign of cancer that is flashed by a change in the size or appearance of a mole. (And, as physicians know, such things can be illogically ignored. People who spot one or more of the indications of cancer stay away from the doctor because they do not wish to have their worst fears confirmed.)

When someone close spends a lot less time with you than before for no apparent reason, a parting is in the offing. When a relationship loses intensity, the same is true. For instance, an intimate friend used to carry on an animated discussion about certain topics. Now you raise and pursue the same topics, but the friend listens with, at best, tolerance, making appropriate responses. An affiliation formerly required you to contribute time, trouble and involvement but gave you things of value in return. Now you seem to have to continue to fill your part of the implicit bargain, but you are short-changed on the income side.

These are some of the signs that may be detected in others. Another important signal is self-conscious behavior. Lovers, friends, colleagues at work once talked freely and naturally with you. Now they act strangely. They avoid certain subjects. You catch them looking at you sympathetically or specula-tively—or trying to ignore you. We are not suggesting that the anticipation of leavetaking requires you to develop para-noid tendencies, constantly asking, "What did he mean by *that?*" We are saying that imminent parting is foreshadowed in the behavior of others, and that one need not be excep-tionally perceptive to see it.

Don't look for the signals of future leavetaking only in others. Look at yourself as well. A relationship takes time. Once you spent that time gladly, now you find it incon-venient and often have something else you'd rather do. In the past you were never bored when you were with a certain person or performing a certain activity. Now you *are* bored. You may feel guilty about it. Being polite, you mask your boredom. Fine; continue to be courteous. But take note, also, of the slackening of intensity in your involvement.

Something similar can be said for your give/take ratio. In the course of a particular attachment you may never have noticed how much you had to give, because you received so much in return. Now the other person may be trying to contribute to you the same things as always, but you do not need or value them as much as before. Moreover, you are conscious of the increasing effort it takes to fulfill your side of the relationship.

Earlier we suggested certain questions that can help you gauge the state of a relationship. Ask yourself the same questions, with particular attention to the degree of change that has taken place in each category. One change in an affiliation —say a moderate diminution of time involvement—need not be significant if the other elements, notably intensity and the give/take ratio, remain as they were. But if more than one factor shows alteration, it is well to consider the possibility that the relationship is moving toward the point of leavetaking.

### Decide on the Leavetakings YOU Need to Initiate

A comprehensive leavetaking strategy goes beyond the matter of identifying the factors that are leading toward the end of a relationship. This is important, but it is still reacting rather than taking the initiative.

In some cases you should be the one who decides to end the association and who orchestrates the parting, even in cases in which, if you did nothing, the relationship would go on indefinitely. This is not cold-bloodedness. It is objectivity. It is one key to growth into further stages of a richly satisfying life.

The well-balanced and conscientious person does not break deep and long-standing associations frivolously. This is something that we do after careful deliberation. But it is folly to reject any such deliberation because of sentiment, nostalgia, dutifulness, or worry about what others will think.

Apply objective criteria to all of the relationships in which you are now involved. If the relationship is solid and meaningful, it will stand the test. If it has lost its validity for you, the time has come to end it.

The strategies incorporated here will help you to break

off such outlived associations and replace them with more fulfilling ones.

## Toward a Strategy of Leavetaking

You have identified an attachment that is changing and diminishing—on your side, on the other side, or both sides. There will be a leavetaking—that is certain. The important next step is to develop a means of dealing with it.

At this point we must offer a distinct warning. Many people are able to acknowledge the signs of approaching leavetaking when they affect relationships that are not vitally important to them or relationships in which their own involvement is diminishing. They cannot, however, accept equally clear signals that have to do with an attachment that is still a very important part of their lives. In a typical incident, a woman—call her Phyllis Winston—began to see that Tess Field, her longtime best friend, was not as friendly as before. The women had known each other since college. They had shared with each other through marriage, the births of children, the move to the suburbs. They were neighbors and still close acquaintances.

Field, however, had begun to act remote. She did not drop by for coffee. At parties she talked with others, avoiding Winston. She no longer seemed interested in the concert series that the two women had attended while their husbands did other things.

At first Phyllis Winston was worried; what could Tess's problem be? Then she was hurt; an old friend was turning her back. At last Phyllis Winston came to see and accept the fact that she and her old friend had drifted apart. Phyllis decided that there was no point in pursuing a relationship that had cooled, for whatever reason. She became involved in different activities, cultivated new friends.

So far so good. But it came as a complete surprise and devastating shock to Phyllis Winston when her husband told her that he and Tess Field were in love with each other, had been for a long time, and now were "going public" with it. It did not matter about the children or what people would say; the two lovers were going to be together. Phyllis Winston's husband wanted a divorce. He added that Tess Field was saying the same thing to *her* spouse.

The signs of this leavetaking were far more obvious in the case of Phyllis Winston's husband than in that of her friend. Phyllis had observed the deterioration of her relationship with Tess. She had completely overlooked the signals that pertained to the much more important relationship.

The significance of a relationship to you—the degree to which it has become an integral part of your life—is no safeguard against leavetaking. People whom we "can't live without" go out of our lives, through alienation, death, or other circumstances, just as people do whose losses we can stand. It is not easy—it is very hard—but you must be as careful in measuring the present state and future course of your most vital relationships as you are in observing the more casual ones.

The fact is that one need not even acknowledge the approach of a particularly painful leavetaking to start building immunity against it. We can begin at any time by making sure our lives do not become closed systems. When we are shut off from contact with new faces and new experiences we are easy prey for all of the most catastrophic effects of parting when it comes.

So it is essential to meet new people; enter different circles; vary the routine. Such behavior has several beneficial effects. It builds up the reservoir of affiliation, so that when a severe leavetaking comes, there are other attachments at hand to which we can turn. In addition, a continuing quest for the new develops flexibility and resourcefulness in forming other relationships. It happens over and over again—a bereaved or deserted person realizes that it is necessary to fill the void but does not know how to do it. By making sure we encounter change, we strengthen our coping mechanisms and tune up the social skills that must be brought into play when we are called upon—as a matter of survival—to form new friendships and attachments.

And, we might add, the receptivity to new friendships and experiences enables us to grow and live to the fullest and most rewarding extent that we can.

This is a general commonsense precaution. There are strategies to be followed when a more particularized leavetaking starts to loom.

FOUR STRATEGIES FOR
SUCCESSFUL LEAVETAKING

THE IDEA OF DELIBERATELY PLANNING and carrying out a leavetaking is not intrinsically attractive. It may seem cold and calculating. But the time comes when it is necessary. Leavetaking is too sensitive and important to be left to chance. The decision to part, and the execution of that decision, involve emotional and rational dimensions. To overlook either is to invite anguish and failure.

Successful leavetaking requires planning. When the time for "goodbye" approaches, we encounter problems and feel pain.

We are not sure we want to make the break.

We hate to give up on relationships in which we have invested so much.

We don't want to hurt others.

We would like to explore all reasonable possibilities of improving the relationship before abandoning it.

We find it enormously difficult to pull out of associations that have become part of our lives.

Here are four strategies calculated to minimize the hurt and expedite the necessary change.

## The "Spacewalk" Strategy

A few years ago we all thrilled to the experience of seeing live television pictures of men in space. One of the most stunning features of the Apollo program was the spacewalk. An astronaut would emerge, slowly and carefully, to float free in the emptiness of the void between the earth and the moon.

At first the spacewalker, awed and perhaps somewhat daunted, remained close to the hatch. Then, as his confidence grew, he would venture farther and farther from the safety of the ship. Finally the full joy of walking in space took hold, and the astronaut went to increasingly daring lengths. In at least one case the commander of the spacecraft had great difficulty in talking the spacewalker back. The journeyer wanted to prolong the thrill of extravehicular activity.

Of course the spacewalker was not floating altogether free. He was still connected to the familiar environment by a safety line and an "umbilical." A human being had gone forth to a completely new experience—while remaining moored to the familiar.

We can use a modification of this concept in preparing for leavetaking. Here's an example of how it works.

Doug and Laura Catherwood have been married for nine years. He is thirty-three, she is thirty-one. They have two children, Ruth, eight, and Andrew, six. Doug is a lawyer. Laura graduated from college and worked while Doug was going through law school. Since then she has devoted herself to the joys of suburban motherhood.

There are times now when the joy seems not altogether pure. The children still take a lot of caring for, of course. There is PTA. There is the local social network, a small but lively system comprising couples of about the same age and status. Laura is keeping busy, but sometimes she thinks that what she has now is not enough.

Doug works hard. Often he has to be away. He brings work home. He and Laura don't talk about things the way they used to. Doug evades conversation about his work. One of his standard lines is, "It's a little complicated. It would take too much time to explain." Laura has been trying to understand Doug's work better so that she can be more adequately qualified as a confidante. That's complicated, and, truth to tell, Laura doesn't find it all that interesting. Occasionally she feels guilty about this.

Their sex life still exists, although it has diminished in frequency and passion. Laura finds this perfectly understandable. Once they were more daring in bed. They tried different things. Laura would still like to try different things; Doug is reluctant. So this phase of their life, like others, has become fixed on a more or less pleasant, if not exhilarating, plateau.

When the Catherwoods go out or entertain, they do it together. When Doug is not home in the evening, Laura waits for him.

The home is Laura Catherwood's spaceship. Outside, it is a whole different world. She feels impulses toward experiencing that world, but she holds back. The world outside is strange. Besides, Laura feels that loyalty requires her to remain in a passive role.

A friend, Jessica Riley, has a suggestion. Jessica, too, is feeling housebound. Why don't she and Laura—and other women they know—make it a point to go out by themselves one night a week? How about Wednesday? As for the men, they can do whatever they want on that night.

This notion has been advanced before, by one friend or another, over the years. Laura has never gone for it. Now she allows herself to be persuaded. She and Jessica, with others, begin to spend time away from their husbands. They go to shows and movies. Then the idea of enrolling in extension courses comes up. Laura decides that she might try this as well.

Doug has never said much about all this one way or the other. He also does not say much about what he does with his "nights off." The Catherwoods have entered a phase in which each one spends some planned time apart from the other.

There are certain things about this arrangement that make Laura uncomfortable. She feels a little guilty about it. Also she feels apprehensive. So far as she knows, Doug has never been unfaithful; until recently the thought had never crossed her mind. But when a wife deliberately says to a husband, "You're on your own"—well . . . Laura has seen and read enough to know what might happen. Nevertheless Laura Catherwood is enjoying her new freedom. As a reaction to it —to some extent because of guilt—she has become more loving toward the children and more affectionate with Doug when they are together. She has a sense of adventure. She is losing some of her inhibitions about pleasure. She has, for example, begun to reintroduce a note of variation and innovation in their sex. Doug was at first amused (with a tinge of wonder and apprehension). He would speculate aloud—not altogether in fun—about what Laura was doing on her own to get such ideas. This has stopped bothering Laura.

Laura Catherwood has embarked on a "spacewalk." She is engaged in *limited leavetaking*, in which she ventures forth into another realm of life without cutting the lifelines to the familiar.

Limited leavetaking involves the sampling, in small doses

at first, of what life would be like—or could be like—after a significant leavetaking. Laura Catherwood does not think of it that way but this is what she is doing. A limited leavetaking is a way of becoming familiar with the positive possibilities of parting. It enables the person to find out what can be good about leavetaking as well as what can be bad about it.

The strategy is a simple one once you have determined that it is a useful idea and have shaken off the inhibitions and guilt feelings that militate against it. Guilt and fear are the biggest barriers to overcome. Limited leavetaking, when first contemplated, can seem like a cold-blooded betrayal. But it is not.

This "spacewalk" strategy can strengthen an existing relationship by enabling the individual to approach the old attachment with a fresh viewpoint and sense of adventure. Sometimes it can lead the person to place a higher value on the familiar association and the familiar way of life. In this sense it is the spice that adds zest to existence.

Granted, limited leavetaking can lead in the other direction. The leavetaker, at first hesitant, becomes bolder, ventures farther. One party to the arrangement ventures farther than the other. One individual concludes that things would be better if the umbilicals were cut altogether.

So there are risks. But these are risks that would be encountered whether limited leavetaking were tried or not. When this strategy is employed, the relationship is, at best, routinized. At worst it may lead to a leavetaking that is cataclysmic for the unprepared party.

Think about a current relationship that has lost its zip and shows signs of wear and tear. Attempting to cling to the arrangement by going through the same routine is not likely to be a successful tactic. It may be time to take your first steps outside the spaceship. You are unlikely to find the alien environment out there totally to your taste. There will be bad experiences. But there will be good ones too.

You will be managing your own life to a greater degree than you did before. You may well discover a new psychological terrain in which you might not want to reside permanently, but which is pleasant to visit. You will be preparing yourself for a leavetaking that might come. If it does develop, you will not feel stranded. There will be other attachments, perhaps tenuous, that you can strengthen and build into a new and possibly better way of living. And even if the leavetaking does not come, you will be living in a different dimension for at least some of the time. This experience can do a great deal to make old attachments and the familiar way of life seem new again.

Limited leavetaking contains risks. The advantages usually make the risks worth taking.

### The "Investment Analysis" Strategy

When leavetaking comes without warning, the loss may appear to us to be much greater than it actually is.

Barbara Strauss had worked for the law firm of Engels, Fleet and Woodhouse for six years. For the past three years she had been Thomas Fleet's secretary. At the time she began to work with Fleet, her predecessor had uttered a dire warning: "You will never get along with him. Nobody can. That's why I'm quitting. He is a first-class, number-one son of a bitch."

Thomas Fleet was difficult, no doubt about that. He was sometimes abrupt. He fussed about petty details. He referred to Strauss as "my girl," as in "I'll have my girl run off some copies for you." He went off for long periods without saying where he could be reached, leaving his secretary with the vexation of coping with impatient inquiries. He dictated in a mumble and scrawled illegible notes. An impossible boss. But somehow Strauss had made things work. She had devised ways to get things done in spite of Fleet's captiousness. She had muted her resentment of his chauvinism. She had even persuaded Fleet to modify some of his working habits. Barbara Strauss was proud of having made an "impossible" relationship into an association that was not idyllic but that worked.

Then Strauss was told that she was being fired. Oh, said Fleet, it was not a matter of any shortcomings on her part. He and the other partners had just decided to make a change. They were going to switch to a word-processing system that would no longer require the services of executive secretaries. They would give Barbara reasonable severance pay, plus good recommendations.

Barbara Strauss was crushed. It was not so much the problem of getting another job; it was, rather, the fact that she had put so much effort into making this job workable. Now, just when her labors were beginning to pay off, the relationship was being severed. Strauss was angry. She stormed out of the office. She returned later to try to plead with Fleet to change his mind. Then she went to Mr. Woodhouse. No satisfaction. She waited and waited and finally got in to see Mr. Engels, the head of the firm. Nothing doing there either.

The parting was ugly and the aftereffects dismal. Barbara Strauss was so discouraged that she made only halfhearted efforts to find another job. On those interviews she did arrange, she spent so much time criticizing her former employers that the prospective boss wrote her off as a risky proposition. Strauss became increasingly embittered.

This sort of thing happens in many leavetaking situations. The individual who is on the receiving end of the bad news finds the association nearly impossible to give up, not because it was so rewarding in itself but because the person has made a large investment in making the relationship function and now feels cheated of the fruits. Worse, the effort and anguish that went into getting the association into shape tend to give the individual an exaggerated idea of the value of the relationship. It's not unlike the shock experienced by people of the Depression years who painstakingly put money, bit by bit, into bank accounts, only to see those banks fail, with the savings irretrievably lost.

Any relationship that calls for a disproportionate initial commitment by one of the parties carries the potential for damage.

Barbara Strauss was betting on futures. She overinvested at the very beginning, with little or no return. She submitted to humiliation. She endured unpleasantness, sometimes insult. She compromised her principles. She figuratively prostituted herself to get a difficult and unappreciative boss to become, not one of nature's noblemen but at least endurable.

In taking this approach Barbara was driven by a complex of motives. For one thing, she was carrying out in action what Thorstein Veblen called the "instinct for workmanship"— the impulse to do a good job even under adverse circumstances. The fact that her boss had practically no inclination to establish a useful working affiliation made her task harder, but she put her whole heart and soul into it.

When we give too much of ourselves to a relationship in the hope of future reward, we court catastrophe. It is quite possible for one person to do this even when the other person or persons involved are by no means inhuman. A youngster leaves home. The mother is devastated. She decries the child's "ingratitude." She is lamenting all of the effort and expense that went into raising her child. All of this, according to the mother, was a kind of investment that was supposed to come to maturity in the form of comfort, love, companionship and financial support. The parent feels robbed.

A marriage fails. The grieving husband is unhappy for many reasons, but one of the principal ones is that he feels he put so much into trying to make it work and he has been repaid shabbily. Something similar happens on occasion when a sudden death occurs. The bereaved individual is *angry* at the dead person. He had invested so much of himself in the other one, and now that one is gone.

The "What a waste!" reaction is a particularly difficult form of leavetaking trauma because the person who suffers from it is made to feel even worse by the knowledge that it is an illogical and unworthy reaction. There is not only anger at the person who has taken leave; there is anger at oneself for "having been such a fool."

To forestall this reaction, it's useful to conduct in the case of any close relationship a kind of "running investment analysis."

How much are you putting into the relationship? How much is the other person investing? What are you getting out of the relationship right now? Are you getting as much as you put in? Or are you paying a very high price to keep it going?

To what extent are you hoping that your "investment" will lead to greater fulfillment in the future? How far off is that future? What are the signs that will show that you are beginning to receive a fairer return? Do you see any of those signs?

How would you feel if the relationship were broken off tomorrow? Would you have pleasant memories? Have you learned from it? Have you grown? Would you be angry and ashamed of having made a fool of yourself?

Such a running analysis can do at least a couple of healthy things. It can draw your attention to a situation in which your part of the association is all outgo and no income. Barbara Strauss was investing time and intensity in a relationship that held few current rewards. Her pride in modest accomplishments and her hope for further change led her to overlook the extent to which she was giving too much and receiving too little.

When you know what you're paying and what you're getting, you can take action. Sometimes all that's required is a reevaluation of the pluses and minuses. Maybe you really need to give as much as you're giving. Maybe you get genuine pleasure and fulfillment from the giving. If this is so, learn to savor your contributions as you make them, rather than considering them to be compulsory efforts which are made only so that you can earn a future reward. Some people go through life collecting Green Stamps and hoping they will be able to redeem them someday. You can't live on a contingency basis.

For example, Nancy Wilcox has begun to wonder why she puts up with her friend Trish Mayo. Trish always seems to have a problem of some sort and is always laying it in Nancy's lap. Wilcox spends a lot of time counseling her friend—on everything from why you don't wash bright prints in hot water to the relative merits of common and preferred stocks. There are times, and they have become more frequent, when Nancy Wilcox feels that she has enough dependent personalities in her own family without having to cope with another one. Nancy's children require a lot of care, and her husband, competent enough on the business side, can't seem to add up a checkbook or replace a leaky washer. "Who needs it?" asks Wilcox as she sees Trish approaching with another dilemma to discuss.

The obvious answer is to cool the relationship with Trish Mayo. But Nancy Wilcox, an analytical person, thinks through the consequences of that action. She starts to see that what she has always considered to be trouble and inconvenience is really a form of psychic income. Wilcox enjoys the role of counselor. She likes to be able to help someone else. She learns from Mayo's problems; some of them are like dry runs which alert Nancy to pitfalls she should look for and avoid in her own life. And Nancy derives satisfaction from the repeated reminder that she is a very "together" individual who can cope with the ordinary and not so ordinary vicissitudes of life.

This kind of rethinking can enable you to place a current relationship in perspective and to remind you of what you are getting out of it. When you are able to place some of the factors of the association on the credit side, instead of putting everything in the debit column, you value the relationship more.

Then, too, an assessment of the running income-and-outgo balance can show you the areas in which you can reasonably expect to get more immediate satisfaction. Because Trish Mayo is so dependent, Nancy Wilcox has fallen into a pattern of never asking anything of her friend. This is counterproductive. It does not help Trish and it vitiates the association for Wilcox. Trish may not be the kind of person one goes to for advice about a sexual dry spell or the strong and weak points of competing brands of automatic dishwashers, but she has qualities of warmth and sympathy that can and should be called into play. When Nancy Wilcox determines to require her friend to contribute more to the relationship, she enhances the friendship for both of them.

But if your assessment demonstrates clearly that the give/take ratio is distinctly against you, and that you are counting on things getting better at some unspecified time in the future, then the red alert has been flashed. It is time to think about assuming the initiative for leavetaking. *You* should be the one who breaks off this unrewarding association.

Finally, even if you examine a relationship, conclude that it is not paying off, and then do nothing to change or end it, the ultimate leavetaking will not be as difficult for you as it might have been. Instead of thinking ruefully of how much you have invested in the affiliation, and feeling foolish for having done so, you can remind yourself that it was not all that good at any point and that you are probably well out of it.

## The "Overhaul" Strategy

There are times when preparation for leavetaking does not lead to full-scale leavetaking at all. Rather, it results in a fundamental change that reshapes the relationship into a form that is new and more satisfying for all concerned.

Ed Mann was going stale on his job. Most of the daily routine bored him; some of it disgusted him. He had been thinking about getting another job, but there weren't too many jobs available for people in his age bracket. Furthermore, he had been at his present company long enough to think about the retirement plans. But that didn't make the job any more bearable. Furthermore, even if Mann felt that somehow he could endure the job, he knew that he was not delivering in the way that he once had. He was uneasily aware that the matter of leavetaking was not entirely up to him. It might be forced on him; he might be fired.

Here is what Ed Mann did. He began to scrutinize every aspect of his work, big and small, asking at each point:

Why am I doing this?

What do I get out of it?

What does anybody else get out of it?

Is there another way to do it?

Does it have to be done at all?

What would happen if I changed it, or even stopped doing it?

Mann's process started with the first tasks of the morning, after he had taken off his coat and sat at his desk. Arrayed before him he would invariably find piles of correspondence: letters, memos and reports that had to be read and sometimes answered. The handling of the correspondence was burdensome, and Mann felt that he was taking longer to do it than was necessary. He was enraged when some interruption—a phone call or a visitor—interrupted this chore. It was difficult to get back into the flow of it.

Ed Mann applied his questions to the problem of the correspondence. They led him to wonder why he had to do it first thing in the morning. With this thought came the awareness that the correspondence routine was occupying him at a time of day when he was relatively fresh and might have been grappling with other problems. He was deferring larger decisions until later, after he had done a lot of detail work, gone to a meeting or two, a business lunch. By then he felt fatigued and unable to cope with topics of broader import.

Well, why was he doing it this way? After sorting through a good many possible answers, Mann had to conclude that he followed his present routine because he had been doing it this way for a long time. It was a habit. There was no rule that said he must complete the paper work before turning to anything else.

Mann made a change. There were certain urgent *In*-box matters that had to be taken care of first thing. These he handled. The rest of the correspondence he put aside for completion during unscheduled holes in his day. He had feared that this would upset his relationship with his secretary. He found that she, too, was bored with the routine and did not mind the change at all.

Ed Mann applied the same set of questions to other tasks— meetings, for example. On examination, some of his optional meetings turned out to have deteriorated into bland routines in which everybody went through the motions without accomplishing much. He cut back on regular meetings, placed the emphasis on calling sessions only when there was reason for them.

Then there was the problem of interruptions. Ed Mann's "door was always open." He permitted himself to be interrupted. Upon reflection, he realized that this practice went back to an earlier day when he had been eager and insecure, afraid of the consequences of making himself unavailable to bosses, colleagues and subordinates.

So now he started to close his door. When someone wanted to break in on his solitude, he would say, "I'm busy now; I'll get back to you." At first he had to force himself to do this. After a while it came more easily.

Mann's zest for his job improved markedly. So did his performance.

By reducing an existing relationship to its nuts-and-bolts essence—asking whether each detail is still necessary or whether it can be changed or eliminated—you can reengineer the relationship. Bonds become needlessly tight when time and routine make us more aware of the bonds than of the reasons for them. Stripping an association to the bone and questioning each aspect of it is a form of *preventing leavetaking*. It enables us to cut away the unnecessary and burdensome aspects of a relationship and to give new life to it by rediscovering the mutual benefits that led to its foundation in the first place.

This does not always happen. Sometimes this sort of bit-by-bit analysis will lead one to the conclusion that there is really nothing left but the routine; the core of the association has eroded. When your examination makes this apparent, the only thing to do is face it. A leavetaking is essential and inevitable. But that leavetaking should be relatively easy to handle, since the process of scrutiny has demonstrated that it has no real substance.

When a relationship is in trouble, look at the details of it.

Forget about the forest and focus on the trees. You may well conclude that a process of pruning and transplantation can build a new and better relationship. Even if it does not, you will have shown yourself how little remains and how necessary it is to take leave.

## The "Habit" Strategy

Associations become habits. We occasionally involve ourselves in relationships to the point of addiction. Leavetaking becomes very difficult. The "withdrawal symptoms" may be agonizing, and the anticipation of them causes us to cling to a relationship that has become unsatisfactory and is moving toward a break.

At work Larry Marks had always been "one of the boys." He and half a dozen other men had started at about the same time, gone through the training program, and followed more or less parallel paths.

They became close friends. They had lunch together. They grouped into an informal society, dubbing themselves— without extraordinary originality—the TGIF Club, meeting every Friday evening for a drink after work. They formed a bowling team. With their wives, they frequently went on weekends together. Often two or more of the couples went on vacation with each other.

This situation had continued without much change for seven years. Without much change, that is, on the surface. Beneath the surface the people were changing. But the TGIF Club remained a strong entity.

Then the paths taken by its members started to diverge. One was fired. Another quit. Two men who joined the company about a year later than the original six were absorbed into the group. However, for four years the "membership" had remained stable.

Larry Marks was ambitious. He also was good at his job. For a couple of years he had been angling for a significant promotion. One important aspect of the promotion would be that Marks would be called upon to supervise some of his TGIF friends.

The possibilities of the promotion began to crystallize. Marks was singled out for praise by the company brass. He had for the last two years received raises which, he was sure, were bigger than those given to his colleagues. But he did not feel entirely happy. His boss had hinted more than once that promotion would mean Larry should spend less time socializing with those he would now have to manage. Larry felt guilty. How could he turn his back on old friends like that?

Besides, Marks told himself, a man could not cut himself off from friends just because he had a bigger job. What he did on his own time was his own business. He made a good case, in his mind, for the feasibility of taking on a management job and still seeing his old acquaintances in the same way that he had always seen them.

This proposition did not hold up. Marks had to admit that his task would be much more difficult if he remained on the same basis of easy friendship with the other club members. Much of their conversation was shop talk, and a lot of it involved casual ridicule of the organization and the shortcomings and foibles of management. Larry Marks could see that, as a member of management, he would be handicapping himself by engaging in such talk. Furthermore, how could he give instructions to people with whom he was socializing during evenings and weekends?

There was another realization, about which Marks felt bad but which he was beginning to acknowledge. The close association with this long-standing circle of friends was not as much fun as it once had been. Larry Marks admitted to himself, with a mixture of surprise and pain, that he was often bored with his old buddies. He was not as interested as he once had been in talking about football, storm windows, kids, septic tanks, and the paraphernalia of social intercourse that had provided conversational topics for a long time.

Marks talked his feelings over with his wife, Lettie. In a way he had been hoping that she would declare it unthinkable that they should ever relax the bonds that had tied them to the others for so long. But Lettie disclosed that she shared some of Larry's feelings. Moreover, she was eminently sensible about the practical considerations involved. She was ready for something different; she was all in favor of her husband's success, and she saw that the TGIF Club was a growing drag.

But breaking off would be hard. The Markses made a few tentative efforts. They made excuses not to join the others on a couple of Saturday nights. There were kidding remarks, some not altogether without a certain edge: "What's the matter, Larry? Getting too good for your old friends?"

Larry and Lettie Marks decided that the leavetaking could not be handled without planning and effort, and that there would be pain and stress. They sat down, discussed the situation fully, and came to a joint agreement that they would cool the relationship.

Having made that decision, they began to put it into effect. Larry, a methodical person, started keeping a written record of the amount of time he spent with the TGIF Club, individually and with Lettie. He had known in a general way that the involvement took a lot of time. He was surprised to find that it was even more time-consuming than he had ever dreamed.

After each get-together the Markses talked over their reactions. They discovered that often they scarcely remembered the details of anything that had been said. Their feeling after a night with the group was nearer exhaustion than exhilaration. In addition, Larry Marks had to admit that he was not infrequently irritated with the limitation and smallness of outlook exhibited by his contemporaries. They just did not talk the same language any more.

One Sunday, after a Saturday-night party, Larry and Lettie were sitting around doing nothing, although there were things to be done. They realized that they had fallen into a pattern of lazing away Sundays after socializing with the others. Lettie said, "Don't let's let ourselves do this. Let's do what we have to do around here, tired or not." So they pulled themselves together and undertook some of the household chores they had been permitting themselves to duck on these occasions.

The next time Larry had lunch with the boys, he forced himself to really *listen* to what was being said rather than switching off most of his mind and making automatic responses. After lunch he thought about the things he could have been doing if he had skipped the lunch, consumed a sandwich at his desk, and made a start on the afternoon's work. That evening he stayed later than usual to do the things that had been left undone.

The Markses continued to take note of the actual details of their social life with the TGIF group. They pushed themselves to perform tasks they had previously let slide after a session with their friends. Their feelings began to firm up. They did not turn against their old friends, but they increased their awareness of just what was involved in the friendship.

Larry bought tickets to some shows on Saturday nights, nights when the gang would ordinarily be gathering at someone's house. The Markses had not gotten out by themselves very much; they found they enjoyed it immensely. Furthermore, they did not have as much difficulty or guilt in saying that they were unavailable.

And gradually Larry and Lettie Marks became less involved with the people they had been so close to for so long. There were difficulties. Some of the others were resentful and made their resentment known. The Markses sometimes endured agonies of guilt.

But the leavetaking was negotiated. Larry and Lettie Marks don't belong to the TGIF Club any more. They have new friends. Larry Marks still sees his old acquaintances of course. He supervises some of them. He got the job. He's happy in it, he is doing well at it, and he and his wife find the new friends they've made more interesting and stimulating.

The Markses broke the habit of a dead relationship by acknowledging it as a habit and doing what was necessary to make a change. It's worth noting that they employed elements of one tactic that can be used even more extensively in certain situations. This is the tactic of *negative reinforcement.*

Negative reinforcement might be called positive nit-picking. When an association becomes a habit, we tend to see only the good aspects of it. If there are few good aspects, we make them up. By negative reinforcement we isolate and focus on one plainly unsatisfactory element of the situation. Once we allow ourselves to admit that there is a problem in this minor respect, it is easier to face the larger drawbacks and move on to the necessary conclusion, whether it is to alter the relationship or end it. One young woman opened herself up to a healthful reevaluation of her relationship with a self-centered and nongiving man by looking—really looking—at the way he gobbled a Caesar salad.

This is not mere nit-picking; nor does it require that the individual avert his eyes from the good things and look only at the bad. The idea is to see the association from a viewpoint that is closer to objectivity. Your job may be in danger. Instead of looking at it as if it were the only source of income available to you, and a source of incomparable satisfaction, look at the frustrations and problems as well. Someone close to you may be drifting away. Instead of idealizing the person, take a good look at the ways in which that person has disappointed you and at the effort the affiliation has required of you. You can benefit from an application of negative reinforcement even in the case of taking leave of a phase of life. You're getting older; you realize that you don't have the vigor that you once had. Rather than bemoan your passing youth, you can spend at least a little time thinking about what you have learned, the ways in which you have grown, and the uses to which you can put increasing maturity. At the same time you can take a look at the difficulties and anxieties implicit in the state of life you are about to leave behind you.

There are flaws in any relationship, and the very fact that you see the beginning of the end of a relationship is in itself an indication of something wrong with it. By looking at all of the shadings of the association, the darker sections as well as the lighter ones, you can build your resistance to the pain of leavetaking, and perhaps conclude that you should take the initiative in making an end of it.

It's not easy to break off long-standing associations. But it may be necessary. A satisfactory life involves growth, which implies a constant search for scope in which to bring your maturing capacities into play and enjoy associations that meet your present needs. You can't achieve such growth when you remain tied to the past.

The essence of this technique for managing a necessary leavetaking lies in these principles:

Register all aspects of the relationship. Make yourself realize the amount of time it consumes and the degree of involvement that it calls for.

Note the extent to which you are enduring the association rather than benefiting from it.

Stop making allowances for the relationship and rewarding yourself for continuing with it.

Start rewarding yourself for every step that reduces your dependence on the old association.

Keep your eyes on the objective: the new and more fulfilling relationship toward which you are headed or the next phase of life that makes it necessary to cut off your involvement with the old ways.

Understand that there will be pangs of pain and guilt. Keep on moving toward the new associations that are vital to your maturity.

As we said, associations are habit-forming. Like some habits, they can be harmful. A person who clings to a habit that should have been outgrown is blocking himself from growth and happiness.

When you identify such a relationship, call it what it is— a habit. Do the things that are necessary to break it. It won't be easy; shedding an ingrained habit never is. But the rewards of being able to stride unencumbered into a richer stage of your development will more than repay you for the effort.

And remember: this is the kind of situation in which the postponing of leavetaking is always worse than the managing of it.

#  PREPARING CHILDREN FOR LEAVETAKING

A SURGEON PREPARES his patient for an operation in this way. He talks with the patient well in advance: "I'm going to operate. I am not scheduling the operation right now, but soon. You will come into the hospital the evening before the operation, which I'll do the next morning. You'll receive normal medication and preparation. The first day you will feel great pain; the next couple of days, moderate pain. Then it will decrease. You will suffer the pain at the time; you will not remember it later. It will take seven to ten days in the hospital, and two weeks at home, for you to be ready to go back to work. You will return to full normal functioning."

This is what the doctor tells the patient well in advance. On the eve of the operation he drops in on the patient, but merely to stroke him. ("The night before, they hear nothing.") The surgeon finds that this approach brings patients back faster. Becoming informed about a stress situation before the full measure of the stress takes effect is the key to the method.

We should prepare children for leavetaking, but too often we don't. How frequently we hear, "Don't say anything in front of the kids."

We try to spare children from pain. One of the ways that we may do this is by trying to keep them from hearing about unpleasant things.

There is trouble. Daddy has lost his job. Mommy and daddy are on the verge of splitting up. Someone close is very sick. A small child wanders into the room, and his mother and father immediately clamp their lips tight and look at him. They are trying to spare him. Instead they make things worse. The child, even a very young child, knows that *something is wrong*. Many children will assume that they are at fault, and will cling to that assumption in the absence of any clarifying information.

Pleasant separation experiences in early life can help greatly in protecting children from the negative effects of stressful separations that come later. By helping youngsters through their first leavetakings we can enable them to begin building positive attitudes that will give them the strength to handle life's more drastic partings.

A well thought out parental approach to leavetaking for children is a kind of psychological vaccine against subsequent traumas.

First, some general principles.

Allow your child to mature at his own pace. Let him test his environment and make mistakes. Encourage him to make his own decisions quite early, starting with his choice of toys, moving on to his choice of clothes and friends. When he makes mistakes, let him recover from them, so that he will develop the self-reliance needed when he no longer has his parents to turn to.

Don't overprotect or exert excessive influence. Babying the

child can lead to prolonged immaturity and fear of the outside world. Your role is one of adviser and resource, not bodyguard.

Most important in helping your child to develop resistance to leavetaking trauma is awareness of your own attitudes. The extreme of indifference or neglect of the child is, of course, harmful. It's equally harmful to become overly dependent on the child for rewards that the parent may feel to be otherwise lacking in his or her life. This engenders excessive emotional dependency by the child on the parent.

Sometimes we try to "lubricate" the child's pain by lavishing on him attention or devotion and by giving him everything he wants. The spoiled child expects to be spoiled by the world at large. The result is frustration and confusion, a feeling of being different from peers, and an inability to establish satisfactory relationships outside the family.

Start early to introduce your child to all available varieties of peer activity; don't wait until he goes to school. Let the youngster make contact with other children; let him choose his friends and experience individual and group relationships. If immediate neighborhood possibilities are limited, turn to nursery school or cooperative play groups as a means of exposing your child to peers. By the time he reaches elementary school he should have learned to adapt to the peer group without immediate access to parental support.

GOING TO SCHOOL. It's the first day of school. The youngster says, "I can't go! I'm sick!" He's not merely acting; he throws up to prove it.

It can be a very traumatic day. If he is unprepared, the child may pretend to be ill or resort to other devices. He may actually become ill.

The likelihood of this happening will be considerably lessened if the child has been exposed to nursery school or play-group experience, during which his mother was absent for at least part of the time. There are other steps you can take to prepare your child for this major event.

Consider your own feelings about it. Parents are apt to have mixed reactions. On the one hand, there may be certain natural relief at the augmented freedom that can be enjoyed with the child in school for part of the day. However—particularly with a first or only child—there may be doubts about the quality of the school, the size of the classes, the character of some of the students, all boiling down to fear about the ability of the child to cope. Some parents worry about the child being underappreciated or ignored. Some may perceive the teacher as competition for the child's love.

Understand your feelings. Having identified them, take care not to communicate any sense of your own anxiety to the youngster. Express enthusiasm and anticipation about the impending adventure. Make a gala occasion out of shopping for school clothes and supplies. Visit the school with your child before opening day, more than once if possible. Many schools have special visiting days for preschool children. The child can meet his teacher and principal, see the door he will enter, be shown where he hangs his coat, where the bathroom is. This helps the youngster, and also the mother, who is better able to visualize her child's experiences when he reports back to her.

Even if the child likes school, he is likely to have some leavetaking reactions. He may exhibit strain and regressive behavior, such as lack of appetite, bed-wetting, irritability and crying. Don't overreact. These symptoms should disappear in a few weeks. If they don't, talk things over with the teacher to see if your child needs extra attention and reassurance. In any event, keep in close contact with the school. By understanding the school's methods and goals you can help your child to adjust.

GOING TO THE HOSPITAL.   A child's trip to the hospital is a leavetaking complicated by parental worry. Here are a few suggestions, based to some extent on a U.S. Department of Health, Education and Welfare report and published as *Your Child From 1 to 12* (New American Library, 1970).

Babies a few months old may not be particularly upset by a short stay in the hospital. The child under three cannot really be prepared for the experience, since he cannot really imagine what it will be like to be away from his parents. For children aged three and older, some things can be done ahead of time.

Talk about hospitals in a casual way. Point them out when you pass them, explain their purpose ("They make you better when you are sick"). Tell the child he was born in a hospital. There are some picture books about life in a hospital, but they don't usually mention the unpleasant aspects. The child should know that while the hospital will make him better, it is a place where he will experience some discomfort and pain.

When a hospital stay is planned in advance, tell your child about it. Don't give him a lot of information at once; encourage him to ask questions. Be truthful without dwelling on unpleasant facts. For the long term it's important to establish trust, and this is done by being honest with the youngster. Reassure him that you will know where he is and will visit him often. Let him know that there will be other children there and that some of them will cry at times and that it's all right for him to cry if he wants to.

Let the child help to pack his things. Include favorite toys or blankets. Assure him that all his things will be in place when he comes back.

Whether the hospital stay is planned or sudden, tell the child why he is going. Reassure him that it is not a punishment for being naughty. Rely on your family and friends to take on your responsibilities so that you can spend as much time with the youngster in the hospital as you can. Stay overnight if the hospital permits it. Take over his care to the extent that you can. If you have to leave, give him something of yours to keep until you return—a book, a piece of jewelry, a comb. Let him express his anxiety, anger or fear. And *don't* expect *him* to reassure *you*. When the child comes home again, be patient. There will be difficult days. No matter how carefully you have handled the situation, he may still feel—for a while—that you have betrayed him and that you can't be trusted. He will require an extra measure of loving reassurance.

MOVING. Relocation, as we discuss elsewhere, may involve severe leavetaking problems for adults. Moving to a new neighborhood or community is, naturally, a different experience for children from that their parents go through. For the parents—or at least for one of them—the impending move often carries expectations of something more gratifying. They can imagine the benefits.

For the child the present is real. The future is vague and hard to imagine. Moving means loss of present satisfactions—friends, teachers, familiar places to play. It is very difficult for the youngster to feel that he can be at home anywhere else. His friends' dismay at his departure may add to his distress, and his parents may be too distracted by the process to give him the attention he needs.

Children need time, perhaps several months, to work through their feelings about moving. They need information and answers to questions about the new home, so that they don't develop misconceptions and unrealistic expectations. They should have a chance to participate in the plans.

Anxiety about moving is most prevalent among younger children. They need reassurance—for example, that their favorite possessions, pets and toys will be moving with them. This is so obvious to parents that they sometimes overlook the fact that it is not obvious to the child at all. In addition to reassurance about these basics of the child's world, point out some of the advantages of the new situation, without trying to paint a picture of paradise. Overselling the new place will backfire in disillusionment and lack of trust.

Respect your child's uniqueness. Every child brings to new situations his own expectations and his own ways of dealing with anticipated pleasures or threats. Encourage the youngster to tell you about his fears; be understanding about his regressive behavior. It takes patience and resourcefulness to make the reasons for the move intelligible to the child, and to help him make his new home into a real and positive image.

Most important in helping a child handle a move is understanding that the child will have fears and anxieties, whether they are manifested or not. The keys to reducing the distress are preparation and participation.

Dr. Gerald Weinberger of Columbia University offers some recommendations.

Tell the child about the move well in advance (rather than keeping it from him until the last minute). Give him time to prepare himself.

Share your feelings with your child. Talk about how sad you feel at leaving friends, but talk also of the excitement of moving to a new place. (This is far better than saying, "Daddy's been transferred and so we have to go.")

If possible, give children a chance to become familiar with the new community. Get pictures and brochures, including pictures of the new house. Visit the new house and the new school. If you can, subscribe to the local paper in advance. This gives parents and children a useful orientation.

Get the children into the act. Let them help with the packing.

Talk with your child's new teacher. This is reassuring to the youngster and informative for parent and teacher.

If there is a choice, try to move at the beginning of summer vacation, to permit the child to become acclimated to the new community before having to cope with the additional challenge of school.

While there is no "best time" to move children, it appears that a move just before the junior or senior year of high school is probably the worst time.

Going to Camp: The First Extended Leavetaking. Going away for a substantial length of time is a focal leave-taking point. It can be a wonderful experience for the child or it can be demoralizing and frightening. Preparation is the key.

Camp day in transportation terminals across the country is a seething mass of crying children wearing paper tags, sweating counselors and harried parents. The stale air resounds with the hoarse bawling of the counselors ("Camp Wink-a-Chickee over here!"), the shrill cries of mothers ("Roger! Your toothbrush!"), and the plaintive wails of the children ("Don't leave me, I'll eat my oatmeal!")

It is a kind of saturnalia of separation anxiety.

The first extended leavetaking subjects the youngster to three powerful terror-producing elements:

The "dark cave" factor. The child is venturing into the unknown. He is about to be pushed into the dark cave. His genes and synapses are bubbling with fright, the legacy of primordial forerunners of eons ago.

The "forever" effect. Small children have not yet developed a sense of measurable future time. "Two weeks" might as well be two years or two millennia. In effect, the child is going off forever.

The "not wanted" syndrome. Abandonment in the woods is a commonplace of fairy tales. To be unwanted by dear ones is traumatic at any age. To the small child it is cataclysmic.

All three of these factors converge on the child when he

first takes leave of home for an extended period. Their effects are often made worse by what is happening inside the heads of his parents.

This is a critical moment for the parent too. Roger's mother is feeling sympathetic agonies at the fear and bewilderment of her little one. She is, also, undergoing an empathic reaction; her own never-resolved fear and anger at being nudged out of the nest have come flooding back. And she is trying to ignore an unwelcome but insistent feeling of relief. Deny it though she may, she will be glad to have little Roger off her hands for two weeks.

At this moment the fresh anxieties of the child and the retrospective anxieties of the parent come together and feed on one another to build up a head of pressure that may never be altogether dissipated. There are immediate effects. The youngsters are mad and scared. The first moments in camp will be a time of stress and compulsive behavior; experienced counselors know that the first night is an orgy of mass masturbation. The parent, guilty and worried, sweats it out at home.

There are short-run effects. When the child comes home he may respond to the enveloping arms of the parent by throwing temper tantrums. He is angry at having been dispatched alone into the dark cave. The parent reacts in astonishment and retaliatory anger. The kid is an ingrate. ("For *this* we sent him to the best place money can buy?")

And there can be long-range effects. A particularly sensitive middle-aged man tells a therapist, "I learned then that you can't count on anybody. Nobody gives a damn. They stuck a tag on me and shoved me into a train. I might as well have been on my way to a gas chamber." Parents who carry the scars of early separation will, in turn, imprint their own children, making the kids into craven wrecks or tiny cynics.

The child will be better prepared to handle extended separation if he has had a chance to spend some time away from home. He can start by spending an occasional night with a friend or relative. After that he can visit relatives who live some distance away. At first these visits should be quite short, particularly for young children.

The next step can be a day camp, especially for youngsters below the age of eight, who are likely to need the nighttime protection of home and family.

The youngster may be reluctant to go away. He should not, of course, be forced. He may lack self-confidence, fear his inability to interact with strangers. Look for the causes of the child's anxiety and try to build up his resourcefulness by reassuring him and encouraging more limited adventures into independence.

When the child is at camp, it's all-important to visit him on visiting day. If he is alone while other youngsters are welcoming their families he will feel severely rejected. Be cheerful; if you have anxieties, don't communicate them to him. When a child has begun to adapt well to the new situation, and sees that he does not miss his parents as much as they apparently miss him, he may develop the guilty feeling that he is doing wrong by being away from his parents and enjoying it.

You may receive tearful phone calls or letters pleading for rescue. Be sympathetic, but assure the child that you have confidence in his ability to make a happy adjustment. It is unwise to react impulsively and bring the child home. Such an abortive experience may have an extremely negative influence on his attitudes toward later leavetakings.

The camping experience is important because it is a measure of how well your child is learning to adapt outside the home. If he comes back and tells of an unhappy experience, don't reassure him and yourself by blaming it on the camp, the counselors or the other children. Evaluate the situation objectively and begin to prepare the child for the next separation.

Again, camp is a leavetaking in which the attitudes of the parents are all-important. Therefore the first necessity is that you face your own true reactions. That's not easy. Ernest Hemingway spoke of the greatest difficulty in writing: "knowing truly what you really felt, rather than what you were supposed to feel, and had been taught to feel." All our lives we are torn between what we are "supposed to feel" and what we really feel. A child is going away. We are supposed to feel boundless love and compassion and miss the child every moment he is gone. Actually, it's a relief; it will be sort of pleasant to have little Roger out from underfoot for a couple of weeks.

There is nothing unnatural or shameful about such a feeling. It is normal and healthy. In fact, when you face it and accept it, it is a lot healthier than the morbid fear that some parents succumb to when the time comes for a child to go away.

For these people the departure of the offspring, even for a limited period, does not represent a natural phase of the child's maturing process. They see the episode in terms of personal loss. It is one more thing that is being taken away from them. The child's absence is a symbol of the empty present and the approaching void.

Such feelings stem from inadequate adjustment to the leavetakings of life. Elsewhere we discuss that problem. Right now let us concentrate on the child's leavetaking difficulties.

You've faced your own reactions. You know how you really feel. The task at hand is to keep from letting your feelings affect your child. The best way to do that is by concentrating on the positive execution of a technique that will reassure the youngster about going away. The essence of the technique is simple. You provide your child with the assurance that he is coming back—and that you want him back—by *concretizing the future.* As we said, the short time-span comprehension of a small child makes him see two weeks as forever. That point in the future, which seems very close to grown-ups, is just not real to the youngster. So you make the future real by providing a "return ticket" by means of role playing.

The "return ticket" is, in effect, the happy ending of the play, complete with props. In this case the happy ending is played before the rest of the play begins. You talk with your child about the specific things that will happen when he comes home: "You'll be on the train with all your friends and with Pete, your big brother. The train will chug-chug through the woods, past the lake, past the big buildings, and then—whoosh!—into the tunnel. You'll be saying goodbye to your friends. You'll get off. I'll be there with a lot of other mommies. A lot of people will be crying. Maybe you'll cry. That's okay. You'll be crying because you had such a good time. Maybe I'll be crying because I'm so glad to see you again. You'll wave goodbye to your friends. We'll get in the car. We'll go by Gombey's for a strawberry ice-cream soda and a double mammoth-burger. And that night—guess what? We're going to the *circus!*"

Use actions and props to support the performance in every way, to make the joyous return a *concrete* event. Show where you'll be standing in the station; sit at the table at which you will sit to eat the soda and the mammoth-burger; show him the tickets to the circus along with an illustrated flyer ("See the picture of the clown?").

WARNING! The "return ticket" must be a *valid* return ticket. It is a dangerous mistake to fake it in any respect.

Faced with a child's distress at leavetaking, we sometimes feel a strong tendency to lie or, as we see it, to say whatever is necessary to ease the pain of the moment. One question here is, whose pain is being eased? We may think we are doing the child a favor. Actually we are assuaging our own guilt and reducing our own discomfort by offering phony reassurances.

Children who receive invalid return tickets don't forget it. They may carry a significant residue of resentment, and all their lives they may find it tough to say the necessary goodbyes or to believe their parents' reassurances.

There are other things that can be done to allay the child's anxiety. For example, have a relative or close friend discuss experiences at camp. Even better, arrange to have the youngster attend a camp at which he already has friends. Tell him what camp will be like and what he will be doing, especially during the first few days.

The temporary leavetaking is a bridge into the permanent and essential leavetaking of a few years later. Acknowledge your own feelings about it for what they really are. Then concretize the return for your child. Make it a real, happy event. And make sure that he receives all that is promised by his "return ticket."

THE DEATH OF SOMEONE CLOSE. Many parents don't want their children to attend funerals or even to hear anything about death. A growing body of professional thought says that this is wrong. Morris A. Wessel, a New Haven, Connecticut, physician, points out that as "he comes to the realization that death implies a permanent loss, a child may be overtly troubled and in deep despair." Dr. Wessel feels that children should be included in the mourning ritual. "To deny a child the opportunity of joining with his family and friends denies him his right as a human being."* This does not mean the child's right to participate in a ceremony; it means his right to work out his own problems of grief and loss. These problems may be more severe for the child than for the adult. Mishandled, they may lead to lifelong difficulties with leavetaking situations.

Children reject the idea of permanent loss. (So do many adults, and it is quite possible that the problems of such

* Morris A. Wessel, in Pine *et al., op. cit.*

adults began in childhood.) Anna Freud and Dorothy Bur-
lingham worked with children whose fathers had been killed
in World War II. These children seemed to understand what
death meant, but they did not accept it. They said their
fathers were dead, then they talked about their fathers coming
back: "I want him to come back. . . . My daddy is big . . . he
can do everything." A four-year-old: "We have to wait until
after the war. Then God can put people back together again."
Another four-year-old: "My daddy is dead. . . . He's in a far-
away place like Scotland."

These comments show how much the children need to
keep their parents alive in fantasy. One might infer that the
children have seized upon comforting things said by other
grown-ups and centered their fantasies around them. What
the children say is heartbreaking. Even worse, it is a danger
sign. If the rejection of the reality of loss goes on too long,
the long-range problems will be far greater than the deep but
temporary pain of permanent loss would have been.

We "spare" children because we want to save them from
pain. But that is not the only reason. We want to spare ourselves the sight of children suffering and the necessity of
dealing with it. We are particularly tempted to do this when
we ourselves are grappling with the agonies of separation.

Some people go to the opposite extreme. They do involve
the child in the ritual of death, but with a panoply of phony
reassurances and sugar-coated ceremony. There is the story
of the father who buys his young son a turtle. The boy is
delighted—but then he says, "Suppose it dies?" The father
describes in loving detail how they will make a little casket
for the turtle, sing around it, proceed with it in solemn
procession to the garden, bury it in stately fashion, and erect
an elaborate headstone. The little boy thinks about all this.
Then he says, "Let's kill it!"

Some parents, on the other hand, use the possibility of
leavetaking as a club. In fact, both parents and children may

use threatened leavetaking as a weapon. Even little kids, when angered, declare that they will run away from home. Some try it. The act is usually more in the nature of retaliation against some perceived parental injustice than the expression of a serious thought of getting away.

A mother, baffled and annoyed, says to her young daughter, "Someday I won't be around any more. Then you'll see. Then you'll wish you had been nicer to me." The threat is less often connected with a major dispute than it is with such an issue as getting a room cleaned up.

The parent who plays on leavetaking fear is reacting out of frustration. The threat is a tactical weapon designed to make the child shut up and act more dutifully. It can have this effect, particularly with younger children; although, repeated too often, its effect wears off.

But the parent who resorts to this ploy does not consider the long-term effect that frequent brandishing of the leavetaking club may have. This parent may be fostering in her child a warped and unhealthy attitude toward parting which can contribute to severe future problems. The child may grow to be a person who suffers from a morbid fear of leavetaking, which may lead either to undue clinging or unwillingness to form any attachment.

### Telling Children About Death

Lifelong reactions to leavetaking may be formed in childhood. One of the most significant moments comes when the child confronts the death of someone close.

Maria Nagey of Budapest studied 378 children to determine their attitudes toward dying. Her findings are significant. She discovered that the youngster of three to five denies that death is final. To him it is like sleep or like a journey. You lie down and die; then you get up again. You take a trip; you return. Sometimes adults are shocked at what they consider to be the callousness of a small child who does not respond to the death of a parent or a sibling. The child is responding appropriately. To him there is no finality involved.

Between five and nine the child begins to accept the idea that someone who has died will not come back. However, he particularizes. He does not realize the universality of death—that it will come to him. This realization grows at about the age of nine.

According to Nagey, children want to know the answers to three questions: What is death? Why do people die? What happens to a person after he dies? For the very young child the idea of death is indistinguishable from the many other goings-away that he experiences every day. Daddy goes to work; mother goes to the store; sister goes to school. He may cry, but the person always comes back. Later he will know that death is different in that the person does not come back.

What we tell a child about dying is obviously conditioned by the child's age. In general, there are a number of principles to be observed.

*Use the correct term.* Say "He is dead" rather than "He has gone away." It is hard to bring oneself to speak of death to a young child, but avoiding the term is no favor. Speaking of death as a "going away" increases the child's confusion. You cannot absorb the shock by euphemism; you can only delay it and make it worse.

*Give a simple but correct reason.* Say "He got old," "He got sick," or "He got hurt." Add that people die when they get old, and sometimes when they get sick or hurt. Don't blame it on God ("The angels took him").

*Offer full participation in the ritual of mourning.* When a child is past infancy it is better to involve him in mourning than to "spare" him. The "sparing" will be perceived as exclusion. Adults and children alike need an appropriate outlet for grief.

*Don't expect grown-up mourning behavior.* While involving the child in the ritual, be prepared for what may seem to be indifference. Allow it, don't rebuke it. Realization of death, and the appropriate behavior, comes at a different pace to children. A boy is dry-eyed at the funeral of his grandfather. Two months later he collapses in tears at the death of his dog. He is mourning his grandfather as well; and he is also mourning for himself.

*Reinforce the idea of continuity.* Let the child see familiar and loved faces around him. Emphasize the pleasures enjoyed in the past with the departed; talk of the good points. Convey the idea that life will go on.

*Be aware of aftereffects.* The child's passivity in the time immediately following death does not mean he has "handled" it. Winston Churchill observed: "The more serious physical wounds are often surprisingly endurable at the moment they are received. There is an interval of uncertain length before sensation is renewed. The shock numbs but does not paralyze. The wound bleeds but does not smart. So it is also with great reverses and losses in life."

# *XXIV* THE MECHANICS OF BREAKING IT OFF

WE DON'T ALWAYS say what we mean. This is particularly true in such an awkward situation as leavetaking. For example:

*What she meant to say:* "We've had a great time together, but now it's over. Let's discontinue our relationship."

What she actually said: "I thought maybe we might want to cool it for a little while. After all, you might have other things to do, and so do I. You know, just take a little break —I don't mean permanently or anything like that. . . . Oh, well, if you really feel that way . . ."

*What he meant to say (to a colleague):* "I'm too busy to spend the kind of time I've been spending with you. Sure, we used to work together, but I've moved up and you haven't, and we just don't have that much in common any more. Besides, it compromises my position to talk shop with you."

What he actually said: "Well, I'm pretty busy, Jack. Don't

you find that long lunches sometimes cut into your time? Anyway, today is bad.... Well, all right, let's get together tomorrow, then, usual time and place."

*What she meant to say:* "Mother, I love you, but I'm married now and I have other priorities. I can't still play the part of your little daughter. It isn't fair to Tom or to me. You really ought to find some other way to spend your time."

What she actually said: "I've got a lot of things to do this afternoon, Mamma, and I don't know what time ... I need to start the supper ... What's up? Can we talk about it on the phone? ... Is it really important? ... Okay, I can't stay for long, but I'll come by around three."

*What he meant to say:* "The car pool has outlived its usefulness for me. Sometimes I'm not sure when I'm going to be able to leave work, and then I have to go through all the business of calling up and getting out of it, and so forth. Besides, these days I'd prefer to drive in on my own. There are things I can think about when I'm alone in my own car, and I can't concentrate when we are gabbing back and forth about the same things we always gab about."

What he actually said: "Sure. Tomorrow morning, just like always."

*What he meant to say:* "We'll both be starting college in the fall. I'm not ready to think about marriage. I don't want to commit myself to one girl. I don't know exactly what I want to do, but I have to be free to find out. We went steady for three years in high school, but now let's stop, at least for a while."

What he actually said: "Yeah, I know, we won't be far apart, but, you know, we'll both be busy.... Okay, I'll call you, and I'll come to see you the first weekend in October."

*What she meant to say:* "I know the committee does important work, but I think I've outlived my usefulness on it. I'm bored stiff with the meetings and the chitchat. I'm resigning."

What she actually said: "All right, I'll be program chairman for one more year, but after that I don't know . . ."

*What she meant to say:* "All we share is a house and a legal relationship. You are satisfied with the setup. You are not going to change. I am not satisfied. I want the chance to change before it's too late. I don't want to live the rest of my life this way. Let's make a clean break of it."

What she actually said: "I know, I know, but you've said that before. . . . Sure we have the children to consider, but they're older now and I don't know if our staying together is the best thing for them any more. . . . Well, then, all right, but things will have to be different from now on."

Many people are able to determine clearly when the time has come to break off associations. They see, with reasonable objectivity, that the parting is a desirable thing, for others as well as for themselves. But they are held back from making the break. It isn't the vision or the will that is lacking, it is the inability to handle the mechanics of leavetaking.

Of course some habitual leavetakers don't worry about this. They don't care how others feel. They are not concerned with tact or technique. They just go. Such individuals have their own problems. Mechanics are not included. But for most of us, to cut off an affiliation is hard. We think about the feelings of others. Often we may exaggerate the effect that our action will have. Years ago one of the authors of this book worked in a small agency run by a fine old gentleman. He received a better offer. After agonized deliberation he decided to take it. But how to break the news? He had been under the old gentleman's wing—"like a son"—and had become a key performer in the running of the business. How could he explain his brutal action in pulling out? And what would happen to the agency?

Finally he bit the bullet. He went to see his kindly boss, and after much hemming and hawing blurted out: "Mr. King, I'm sorry to have to say this, but I've received another offer and I can't turn it down. It isn't that I don't love it here, etc. etc., but I have to think of my family, etc. etc.," and so on for ten minutes of misery.

At last he fell silent. The old gentleman looked at him and said, "Lot of moving around in this business."

That's the first principle in devising a means of taking leave: don't assume that your departure is a death sentence for the people or institutions you are leaving. They will survive.

As a matter of fact, if the relationship has become unrewarding for you, it is probably unrewarding at the other end as well. That may not be immediately apparent to the other person but as you reduce the involvement, it is apt to become clear. But don't use it as an excuse; don't use the old ploy, "You deserve better than me; I'm no good for you."

You may make the break sudden or gradual. The important thing is to stick to your purpose. Anticipate that there will be pain, but don't try to reduce the pain—your own or somebody else's—by hedging, backtracking or fudging.

Perhaps the best way to plan for a successful termination of a relationship is to start with the climactic moment at which the break is made and then work backward.

Most leavetakings involve a confrontation; few of us are able to just walk out. The moment comes when one person says to another, "It's over," and then sticks to it. This is where many leavetakings that should happen get sidetracked. The would-be leavetaker cannot bring himself to the point of confrontation—or, if he can, loses the thrust of his resolution. He permits himself to be talked into continuing the association, or he talks himself into it.

In 1936 the dramatist John Howard Lawson published *The Theory and Technique of Playwriting,* a text that had great influence on many playwrights of that time. Lawson's central concept was that of the "obligatory scene," the crucial moment of the play toward which all the preceding action inevitably must lead. The playwright, Lawson said, starts with the obligatory scene, shapes it exactly the way he wants it to work, and then molds the rest of his play so that this scene is satisfying and inevitable.

If you have determined that leavetaking is necessary, the confrontation at which the break is made is your obligatory scene. You have already done the groundwork. You have analyzed your present and future needs. You have examined the elements of the relationship and identified those that are unsatisfactory and unlikely to become more satisfactory. You have thought about the kind of leavetaking you wish to initiate. You have built your strategy.

Now. "Write" the scene. The cornerstone of the scene is your crystal-clear statement of what you are going to do: "I am going away to take a job in Denver" . . . "I am starting divorce proceedings" . . . "I can no longer participate in this activity" . . . "I quit."

This is central. You must say this, with meaning.

Of course it is not a one-line scene. First comes the "rising action." You lead up to your climactic statement, not to give it greater dramatic effect (although dramatic effect is not inconsequential to the establishment of belief and conviction) but to prepare the way and put the leavetaking declaration in context, lest it be considered a transitory outburst.

Begin by stating the theme: "I've been thinking about our life together." Foreshadow the climax: "And I've come to a decision." Present the framework: "We don't talk with each other any more. We have grown apart from each other." Support the detail: "You come home late from the office at least two nights a week, usually more." (State the details factually and objectively, not as accusation. You are not saying the other party is a bad person; you are describing what has happened.)

Then you make your declaration. Be prepared for the "descending action" which follows: surprise (real or feigned), shock, anger—and, all important, efforts to get you to change your mind.

The key to successful execution of the mechanics of the leavetaking confrontation is sufficient preparation to make sure that you will not be sidetracked. The obligatory scene must be played out. At the end the other person (who is, in terms of dramatic theory, both antagonist and audience) must be convinced.

So *rehearse* the scene. Role-play it over and over again. Think of all the things the other person will say: "You can't leave me high and dry, you have an obligation." ... "Let's give it another try, and I promise this time things will be different." ... "What am I going to do?" Do not feel compelled to provide comprehensive answers for all of the problems, objections and protests you will hear. You cannot solve others' problems for them. In the effort to do so you will only fail to solve your own—or, worse, you will be turned aside from the solution you know is right for you.

Rehearse so that you are able to respond to what the other person will say, and then get the *obligatory scene back on the track.* Your overwhelming priority is to play the scene out.

Effective actors do not just read lines. They understand themselves; they anticipate the factors that may keep them from full success in a scene. Anticipate the emotions and doubts that will beset you at the climactic moment.

One deterring factor that you are likely to encounter is the human impulse toward saving rather than discarding. As we have discussed, we all share this impulse to some degree. Certain people, of course, are possessed by it to extremes. They can never break off anything or throw anything away. A couple visited the home of a recently deceased uncle who was a notorious saver. The house was filled with neatly labeled boxes: "Flashlight Parts," "Bulbs—Working," "Bulbs—Not Working," and so forth. In one corner they found a box marked "Pieces of String Too Short to Save." Sure enough, it was filled with bits of twine a couple of inches long.

After mature deliberation you have concluded that the relationship no longer works. A relationship is not a box of string. To hang onto it when it no longer works is to keep yourself from forming relationships that do work. In preparing for the obligatory scene, anticipate the urge toward saving and be ready to resist it.

There are few of us who want—except in the heat of passion—to hurt others. There are few of us who don't want to be thought well of by another with whom we have had an association. In getting ready for the leavetaking confrontation, admit that, if at all possible, you would like to leave the other person feeling good. Admit this—and then assign to this feeling its proper priority. It is not the most important thing. The most important thing is the successful execution of the needed leavetaking.

Here it is worth while to look at the confrontation as a negotiation. The essence of the tactics of a successful negotiator is that he determines beforehand the necessities—those things he must absolutely come away with. Then he identifies the desirables—the things that would be nice to have but are not essential. The other matters are game pieces to be used as trade-offs. Since the good negotiator does not wish to humiliate or devastate his opponent, he will shape his tactics toward achievement of all the necessities and as many of the desirables as possible. Often he will trade off a desired point for the more desirable result of giving the opponent something that he can regard as a plus, getting the opponent to feel reasonably cordial, or at least enabling the opponent to save face.

Your necessity in the confrontation is the leavetaking itself. You want the other person to understand that it is really happening. You may want the other person to do certain things to facilitate the break, or at least not make it more difficult than it has to be.

That is your "bottom line." The rest you may regard as possible trade-offs, to help the other person or at least make him feel better about things. Don't uncover all of your cards right away. Having determined your trade-offs, withhold them until they can be introduced most effectively as quid pro quo or lubricants to ease the friction. If, for example, there is money or property involved, hold back on your predetermined final concession until it can have the greatest impact. If you have set as your goal a partial leavetaking, you may want to broach the topic of a complete break, then appear to compromise by arriving at the point at which you wanted to be in the first place. Even if there are no trade-offs of any substance that can be offered, you can be generous with acknowledgment of what the relationship has meant to you and assurance that you will be helpful wherever possible (such help, of course, to stop short of drawing you back into the old association).

All this may seem cold-blooded. It is. The climactic scene of leavetaking is not to be played out in the heat of emotion. The decision to break it off must be rational. Once made, its execution has to be carried through with cool determination.

The determination to end a relationship is not to be taken lightly or without clear thought. Once you are sure it's the best thing, plan the obligatory scene; rehearse it; and play it out to the desired conclusion. Failure at this crucial and difficult moment will be calamitous for everyone involved.

# *XXV* DEALING WITH LONELINESS

ATTACHMENT IS A NORMAL ELEMENT of human behavior. We form bonds. The traumatic breaking of these bonds will result in a syndrome of grief—shock, protest, guilt, anger and sadness. As we have said, there is a psychic healing process that goes to work within the healthy individual. It will in time deal with the syndrome of grief if it is not interfered with. Sometimes a person will become embedded in one or another of the stages of the healing process. Sometimes one constituent of the syndrome—anger, for example—will so dominate the reaction as to throw it out of balance. We have discussed the ways in which we can handle ourselves so that the immediate effects of traumatic leavetaking may be overcome.

There remains loneliness. This is a longer-range result, which is not susceptible to the same healing process. Loneliness is the reaction to the *absence of the valued relationship* rather than to the *experience* of the loss. Every other aspect of grief may subside as time goes on, but as long as no new relationship is formed to replace the one that is lost, loneliness continues.

So the remedy for loneliness is different from the remedies that can be applied to other manifestations of traumatic leavetaking. Shock and anger are emotional reactions; they may have little or nothing to do with the objective circumstances. Loneliness is both emotional and situational; it causes psychic pain, sometimes acute pain. But it is directly linked to the situation of lack of replacement of the association.

With loneliness comes a drive to dispel the distress by forming a new relationship or restoring the lost one. The choices made by the bereaved person are most important. As we have seen, a hopeless quest for the reintegration of the former bonds leads to deeper misery. The individual who attempts to find an exact facsimile of the lost object, instead of investigating different kinds of relationships that will meet his present needs and conform more exactly with reality, will be increasingly frustrated and remain lonely.

When we put it in one way, the answer to loneliness is simple. The lonely are driven to find others. When they find others, they are no longer lonely. But it is not just a question of finding others; we must find the *right* others. Otherwise the desolation endures.

Here it is vital to understand that there are different kinds of loneliness which respond to different remedies. Dr. Robert S. Weiss (*Loneliness—The Experience of Emotional and Social Isolation,* M.I.T. Press, 1973) has identified two general types of loneliness. One is called the *loneliness of emotional isolation,* which appears in the absence of a close emotional attachment.

The other type is *social isolation,* the absence of an engaging social network. The network may consist of friends and acquaintances, relatives, colleagues in an organization.

Emotional isolation is caused by the lack of an intense and

sharply focused association, typically a relationship with one person with whom we are very close. Social isolation exists when we are not part of a pattern that brings us into satisfying contact with an adequate number of people. In the social network we do not form the kind of intense bond that is formed in the emotional person-to-person situation.

The individual who has experienced a traumatic leavetaking may suffer either emotional or social isolation or both. The person who is distressed by just one type of loneliness may mistakenly try to resolve the problem by concentration on the remedy for the other type. For instance, the woman who has lost a dearly loved husband may attempt to relieve her loneliness by meeting lots of new people or throwing herself into work. The man who is cut off from a job he has held for many years may try to fill his needs by intensifying his relationship with his wife, son or daughter or a particularly close friend.

In his studies of the lonely Dr. Weiss has found that the lonely human being cannot find a satisfactory answer for one kind of loneliness by resorting to the cure for the other type. The person who suffers from emotional isolation will overcome the distress only through the integration of another emotional attachment or the reintegration (if that is possible) of the one who has been lost. This fact is constantly being realized by separated men and women who become involved in such organizations as Parents Without Partners. New members are attracted to the organization in the hope that membership will lessen their feelings of isolation and abandonment. Within the network they may form new friendships or take on new responsibilities, but unless they also form a single intense relationship, one that provides the same psychic income as the lost marriage, they remain lonely.

Conversely, the loneliness of social isolation can be remedied only by involvement in a social network. This has been demonstrated in studies of couples who move to another area. The wife tends to have "newcomer blues." Her husband has his job; the wife must find her own network. She feels out of place, homesick for the community she has left.

The research shows that no matter how close the marriage or loving and sympathetic the husband, he can be of little real help in such a situation. The wife welcomes his sympathy and attention, but she remains lonely, and perhaps she wonders why.

She needs access to a *network,* typically a network of other women, with whom she can talk about things of common concern. Her husband may have experienced some distress at the move, but he has a steady-made network with which he can connect.

How can we tell whether we are suffering loneliness primarily because of emotional isolation or of social isolation? One clue, of course, lies in the nature of the lost relationship. If it was a sharply focused affiliation with one person, its sudden absence tends to lead to emotional isolation. If it involved acquaintance, friendship and mutual effort with a larger number of people, the loneliness that follows its disappearance is apt to be social in nature.

There are other guidelines. The symptoms of emotional deprivation are in the main different from the symptoms of social isolation, although both are likely to be characterized by the same pervasive restlessness and longing to replace the lost relationships. The symptoms associated with *emotional* isolation strongly resemble the distress of the young child who fears he has been abandoned by his parents: panic, apprehension, anxiety. The symptoms that identify *social* isolation resemble those of the child whose friends are all away: boredom, feelings of exclusion, the impression that one does not count.

We see a thread in the loneliness of adults that runs forward from childhood. The reactions of grown-ups may have been modified by the strength and understanding that comes with maturation, but they still seem to be like the childhood syndromes in fundamental ways. Those who are suffering emotional isolation appear—sometimes very strikingly—to reexperience the anxiety produced by feelings of abandonment as a child. In a sense the lonely are children again. And, like children, they may sometimes look for the wrong ways to assuage their feelings. The person suffering emotional deprivation is jumpy, cannot concentrate, can't read or watch television. He is driven into some kind of motor activity to get rid of his jumpiness. From this he may move on to behaving as if activity is the answer, when it is not.

Not very much is known about the type of person who can best tolerate loneliness. In fact, there are differing hypotheses, each of which seems plausible. It can be argued that the person least affected by loneliness is one who is distant and cool and avoids close attachments in the first place. On the other hand, we may argue that loneliness is least threatening to the mature and self-trusting person who has outgrown his infantile needs and fears. There may be different sorts of capacities for dealing effectively with loneliness, some defensive and some not, but we have little relevant data.

We cannot look forward to a time in life when loneliness is no longer a threat. In fact, as we get older the risks increase. Older people require emotional and social relationships. As time goes on, they stand in greater danger of losing them through the growth and leavetaking of children, their own and their friends' changing circumstances, the necessity of retirement from a job, and death. Loneliness seems to be intrinsic to the human condition. We can reduce it to a tolerable level, but there is an irreducible minimum below which we cannot go.

The best way to reduce loneliness is to form new relationships with the same significance as those that have been lost: intense associations to resolve emotional isolation, the joining of satisfying human networks to reduce social isolation. There is a great danger that the individual may be rich in one kind of relationship and poverty-stricken in another. A person may have a world of friends and a responsible and challenging job and yet be desperately lonely because he lacks a single emotional object. The person who enjoys a rich and satisfying love partnership may be starving for social attachments. Worse, the profusion of good fortune in one area can blind us to the need for sustenance in the other. We think, What's wrong with me? I have many friends [I have my wife or husband], so why am I anxious? It can't be that I'm lonely. And we try to help ourselves by looking for the wrong answers.

While there is a distinct difference between emotional and social isolation, and while the lonely person should try to determine which is his problem, there are in many cases practical considerations that channel our efforts to cure loneliness into what is, at first, not the appropriate channel. An individual loses a close relationship with another person. The bereaved person is suffering from emotional isolation. It can be resolved only by the formation of another close emotional relationship. How can this be done? A range of options must be opened up. As a practical matter, this frequently can be done only through the broadening of one's involvement in a *social* network. A newly widowed woman needs an emotional partner. She joins Parents Without Partners. The social manifestations of that network will not fulfill her needs, but they give her the chance to meet someone who will fill them.

So the road to the reduction of emotional loneliness may lead through the social network. This is proper as long as it is considered a mechanism and not an answer. The joining of the social network has one primary purpose: the ultimate provision of a personal relationship. If the individual loses sight of the goal and tries to make the social affiliations replace the lost emotional bond, the loneliness will go on.

But it may take a long time to form new relationships to replace those that have been lost. Sometimes it is impossible to accomplish this satisfactorily. What do we do about our loneliness in the meantime?

In the short run, the first task is to identify the kind of isolation from which you are suffering. The second task is to take the proper steps to deal with it. At the same time it is necessary to tolerate the loneliness that is inevitable. You hope it is temporary, but it may last a long time.

To tolerate loneliness does not mean learning not to feel it or becoming so used to it that you stop trying to find solutions. It means acknowledgment that being lonesome is something that we must all endure at some time or other. It means responding appropriately—continuing to pursue logically chosen objectives but forbearing to react in panic or self-disgust. When the evening comes and there is no one to be with, then the mature person accommodates to reality by reading, working or watching television. If it is absolutely necessary to make a human contact, write a letter or call a friend who will understand. These things are palliatives, not solutions. Sometimes we hate ourselves for having exposed our weakness by doing them. Mature reaction to loneliness requires that we be generous toward ourselves and not indulge in self-rebuke for reactions we cannot help.

When we are depressed by loneliness we tend to scorn positive thoughts because they are clichés. This is unwise. Things can get better. Loneliness, if one is doing intelligent things to resolve it, is not crippling. To say that things can get better does not make them better, but it is nevertheless important to keep this strong possibility in mind. It helps us to keep on doing the right things that will lead eventually to a satisfying outcome, rather than resorting to panicky measures or lapsing into apathy.

In handling social isolation the solution is to locate a network of congenial people and manage to stay in touch with at least some of them long enough to establish one's own membership. This can be done by setting up social occasions with people met through work. Another route is participation in such affiliations as newcomer clubs, church groups, classes or special-interest groups. At first, in any such association, there will be a feeling of being shut out. Older members of any group will not open up warmly to a newcomer right away; this is as true of humans as of lower animals. But the apparent aloofness is not rejection. The danger is that it will be taken to be rejection by the individual who is sensitized by leave-taking. Selection of the right network, patience and persistence are paramount in combating social isolation.

It is more difficult to handle emotional isolation. As we have said, a social network may provide the mechanism through which a new emotional attachment can be formed. But this can be long in coming. Moreover, it cannot be arranged in the same way as a social involvement. Nor can it be forced. We can do many things to position ourselves so that we are ready and available for a new emotional relationship, but the creation of such a relationship is not a matter of pure volition. Some people make their situations immeasurably worse by trying to force close bonds upon others who are unwilling or unready for them. The effort fails. The lonely person is ashamed of himself for having tried, and he tends to despair of the possibility of emerging from the shadow of isolation.

The active search for an attachment figure can be distressing and demeaning in itself, and its chances for success are dubious. If one works at the search, there are likely to be meetings, dates and involvements, but the relationship that develops is usually superficial and fragile. The outcome is likely to be further loss and a deeper loneliness. Even while one of these forced relationships endures it is hardly apt to be satisfying, because, while it may possess many of the surface manifestations of a satisfying association, it is essentially a fake.

In most cases, the more widely the net is cast, the more

sparse the catch is likely to be. A far-out search for emotional attachment may facilitate sexual adventure, but it provides little in the way of trust or fulfillment. Someone who has been introduced by a friend or perhaps met through work on a political campaign may at least share some values and commitment sufficient to sustain more than a few conversations. Picking someone up at a singles bar is far more likely to result in a brief and unsatisfactory encounter. When one focuses exclusively and strenuously on finding an emotional object, the prognosis is poor.

It is not good strategy to attempt to deal with emotional loneliness by trying directly to replace the lost love object. But this does not mean that nothing can be done. A more appropriate strategy is to give oneself the opportunity to have a satisfying relationship *happen*. This may well be through participation in one or more social networks, even though that participation does not bear directly on the problem. The energy that might be spent fruitlessly in a frantic search for love or close partnership is better applied to the development of the inner resources required to deal with loneliness. Sometimes we can do this on our own. Sometimes it is best done by talking with a friend, counselor or professional therapist. The objective of such contacts is not the formation of an emotional association with the counselor, but rather the help of a sympathetic and experienced guide who may assist us to rediscover our resources, develop them, and bring them to bear on our loneliness.

Accept the fact of loneliness. Build your resources for dealing with it. Identify the kind of loneliness that assails you. Resolve social isolation by becoming involved in the kinds of networks most likely to offer fulfillment. Be open to the formation of an emotional relationship if that is what you need, but don't force it. Remember that under the pressure of loneliness we tend to lower our standards. We accept what we would not accept in other circumstances, and the results are usually unsatisfactory. When a new emotional association becomes a possibility, let it develop naturally.

The most valuable thing you do when you are undergoing a period of intense loneliness may be learning to live with it. You will of course take the right steps to form the kind of relationship that will end your isolation. With patience and luck, this will happen, and your loneliness will be dispelled. But few associations, even the most soundly based and satisfying ones, are altogether permanent. Some time in the future you will probably be lonely again. When that time comes, the effort you have put into coming to terms with loneliness and living with it while you work to solve it will stand you in good stead.

Here are some recommendations to consider.

Differentiate social isolation from emotional. The former is transient; treat it like a stranger at the door. The latter is more like a house guest; it will stay a longer time.

With regard to social isolation, seek out relationships—in church and its activities, in clubs and fraternal organizations —and your roots will soon become easily established in the new soil. Even finding a new barber or beauty parlor that you can call your own will help. Social isolation is cosmetic. Relieving it just means changing the label on the can.

However, when it comes to emotional isolation, the opposite therapy is required. Never rush into the danger of superficial interactions such as those found in clubs or social groups. This will make the cancer of isolation spread rather than become encapsulated. Stay only with small known groups of similar interests. Also, keep your aspirations with regard to permanent associations at a very low level. Don't seek an immediate replacement for your lost object because it won't happen rapidly. However, by keeping your aspirations at a low level, something might develop in time. If you become too eager for a replacement, you may only end up with unfilled expectations, which result in anger and more depression.

# *XXVI* RX FOR THE SUDDENLY ABANDONED

YOU HAVE SUFFERED a leavetaking. Someone close has gone, through death or separation. Right now the healing process is trying to work inside you. It needs help. There are ways in which you can facilitate your recovery, ways in which you can keep from impeding the process, ways by which you can avoid trouble later. Here are some of the elements of your psychological survival kit.

Let your friends make things easier for you. They want to help. Let them provide you with appetizing food and diverting small talk. Take advantage of their offers to entertain you. Slough off onto them some of the most irritating details of day-to-day living—cleaning the house, for example. Call upon a friend when you need something. Make demands.

By using a friend in this way you help your friend and yourself. Friends need to feel that they are doing *something* for you. They appreciate direction. By indicating what you need, you channel their efforts into areas that do you some real good in easing the immediate pain.

But don't call on friends to do more than they are capable of doing or are qualified to do. The most well-meaning acquaintance does not become a professional counselor simply because the need arises. Some bereaved persons pour their hearts out to casual friends and acquaintances. This causes immediate problems and may lead to long-term embarrassment. The first unhappy effect is that the friend is made uneasy by the load of confidentiality and feels inadequate to handling the situation. Nevertheless he may try to offer advice. It may be bad advice. If you are sufficiently objective you reject the advice, which hurts the friend. It's worse if you accept the bad advice.

Even if there is no advice involved, you may squirm later on when you remember all of the intimate information you poured into a friend's ear in the post-leavetaking agony. You will wish you could take the words back, but there is no way to do so.

Unless you have been in the habit of confiding in someone close to you on many occasions in the past—a person who is an experienced listener and who can offer sound advice—you should resist the temptation to thrust a friend or relative into a role for which he is unsuited.

Let your friend help by doing things for you. If you need to pour out your heart, go to a professional counselor. This may be a clergyman, a psychologist, a psychiatrist, your physician. You don't have to know the experienced counselor extremely well to make use of him in this way; in fact some degree of remoteness helps. The screen between priest and penitent in the Catholic rite of confession serves this purpose.

Expect sympathy from your close relatives and friends. Let them turn that sympathy into helpful action that soothes and makes the immediate moment a little easier. To unburden yourself of pent-up angers, resentments and guilts, talk with someone who has experience and qualification in this role.

Don't oversedate yourself. People in torment may be drawn to the bottle, whether it contains pills or booze. You can dope yourself into a state in which you do not feel anguish, but you accomplish nothing and risk much. The work of mourning does not proceed while you are unconscious. It resumes only when sedation wears off, and that resumption may be more painful because of the added burden of guilt you may have incurred by resorting to drugs. Furthermore, the deadening of pain by artificial means may feed on itself and become a habit. By taking the easy path of self-sedation we endanger long-term health, physical and psychic.

Should I tell the children? And how much should I tell them? When children are on the scene, these questions occur to the leavetaken.

A general answer is that children, even the youngest, should be told *something*. They will not be unaware of the atmosphere of anguish and depression. If they are kept in ignorance of the cause, they will invent their own reasons. Often a child will supply reasons that make him take on guilt.

So be honest with the children. "Mommy has gone away." ... "Your father and I are getting a divorce." The amount of detail is a matter of the child's age, emotional resources, and the situation.

Be factual. *Do not* burden children, even those on the brink of adulthood, with your rage and fear. Say "We loved her and we'll miss her." Don't say "She did not love you enough to stay with you."

Work on acknowledging reality. Don't fight to keep the thought of what happened out of your mind. Permit yourself to replay it the way it really happened, not the way you'd like it to come out. Say to yourself, "It happened. It can't be undone." Say it until you believe it.

Don't look for scapegoats. Anger—at yourself, at another, or at both—is natural. You can't avoid the anger, but you can try to keep it transitory, rather than giving it focus and permanence.

We tend to ask "Why?" when leavetaking occurs. We can almost never know the complete answer to "Why?" And having only partial answers, we twist them. We blame ourselves too much, or somebody else too much. Or we turn our fury on third parties, or on God, or on the world in general.

As soon as you can, replace the "Why?" with "What?" Stop looking for causes and begin to think about next steps. Ask "What do I do now?" By doing this you do not magically dispel the grief, pain and anger. But you help the healing process by shifting the ground from purely emotional responses to situational ones—that is, questions that deal with future actions. At first the answer to "What do I do now?" may be "Nothing." Again that's normal. You have no alternative at the moment except to let the work of mourning take its course.

However, very soon you must resume the threads of your life. Start considering the questions of what you do. You may want to begin with small questions: "What will I wear tomorrow?" "What will I have for breakfast?" Move on to the larger issues—not "How do I replace what was lost?"

Pain is part of the process. Accept it. It will be bad, but it will not be too bad to endure. Help yourself to bear it by remembering that the hurt is a by-product of the healing process, like the pain you feel when a broken bone is knitting.

Give yourself solitude. You can't be with someone else all the time—although well-meaning friends may want to keep you company every waking moment. When you're alone, let your mind run free. When it ranges over the leavetaking, let it range. Don't fight it.

Remind yourself of your worth. Leavetaking is not an indictment of you. Of course you are not perfect. No doubt there are things you could have done that you did not do. This is true of everyone. You can learn from the experiences so that you make your next relationship a better one. But one of the big dangers right now is that you will be too tough on yourself. Give yourself a break.

Adjust your time frame. Accept the fact that healing takes time. There are things you can do to help it along, but beyond that you cannot rush the process. You may say to yourself, "I wish I could go to sleep until it's next year." Fine; that shows you know things will improve. But the process has to wend its way through its various steps, and it won't do that while you're unconscious.

Be ready for relapses. You will wake up one day feeling good, and you'll think it's all over. It's not. Later that day you may feel a vivid flashback of agony. Don't let this throw you into despair. It is a promise, not a sign of disaster. The process is working. The engine of psychological well-being is turning over a little, but it is not yet running smoothly. Take your setbacks in stride, and avoid taking on more than you should take on because you think you're fully recovered. The curve of the healing process has ups and downs. You are all right as long as the general trend is upward.

Take good care of yourself physically. There is always a relationship between physical and emotional health. It's particularly important in times of stress like this. You need rest. Lie down even if you can't sleep. Part of you may be reliving the past, but another part will be relaxing. Exercise. Physical effort helps you to rest better and stimulates the positive elements of your mind.

Engage in routine activities rather than heavily challenging ones. You are not ready for major decisions. To the extent possible, defer them or let trusted others make them for you. Handle the minor chores. They will not blot up the pain, but they will keep your emotional and intellectual muscles in tone.

Accept temporary tenderness. People will rally round, even people whom you don't know very well or who in normal times are not very close to you. Take and benefit from the exceptional caring that they offer. Don't expect it to be permanent, and don't hold it against them when, afterward, your relationships with them cool down. They will have served a good purpose when you needed them.

Introduce change into your life. At first make it a small change—a new blouse or tie, a house plant, a book, a hitherto untried recipe. Novelty diverts the anguished mind. Sterility tends to embed you in an early stage of grief for longer than you should remain there. The sampling of little changes will gradually condition you toward the acceptance and seeking of bolder change.

Fix on what is really important to you in the relationships that remain. No leavetaking wipes out everything. Look at what is good in what is left. Appreciate and develop the bonds with the people who are still with you, without using them as a crutch or expecting them to replace what has been lost.

Close the book on the past. There will be wistful moments when you think that it is possible to go back and recover what has been irretrievably lost. Accept these thoughts for what they are—stray by-products of the healing process. Don't try to go down any of these paths; they are dead ends.

Keep souvenirs in their place. You should not try to obliterate all mementos of the old relationship, nor should you brood over them. Put them away somewhere. Later on, when your emotional strength has returned, you may want to look at them. The purpose of a memento is to help you to remember with pleasure and live *today* better.

When you are angry, vent your anger. Cry. Scream. If there

is someone very close whom you trust implicitly, it's okay to have company when you ventilate your rage. Otherwise do it in solitude. Stride up and down. Punch the overstuffed chair. But don't take your anger out on anyone else. Stay away from the phone. If you have to write something, don't mail it.

Record your healing process. If you keep a diary, or find it helps to write things down, fine. But you don't have to put it in writing. The point is to keep mental tabs on how you are doing. In this way, when bad moments come, you can look back and say, "Yes, today is rough, but look how far I've come."

Don't let others dictate how you should act or feel. The grieving process works differently with everyone. Others may think—and let you know that they think—you are grieving too much or not grieving enough. Forgive them and forget about it. By trying to force yourself into a mold created by others or by society as a whole, you stunt your growth toward restored emotional health.

Don't hold grudges. You don't have to lavish long-distance affection on a departed person who has caused you pain, but hating him will only make you feel worse. And beware of the pain that you may inadvertently give to innocent persons in your rage and grief. Remember—and apologize.

When the first pain has subsided, reestablish control of your destiny. For a time you have given yourself over to grief and let others do things and make decisions for you. Now you take over.

Identify the things you need most from a new relationship: love, security, physical pleasure, activity, comradeship. Look around at the ways in which these needs can be met. Think about whether you are suffering from emotional isolation or social isolation or both. Don't go all out for one when you need the other. Look for the kind of new association that will fill the vacuum and enable you to grow.

Sample, don't plunge. A range of new experiences is open to you. Avoid the tendency to pursue single-mindedly the first possibility that comes along. Keep your options open.

Build on the positive past. Renew and strengthen those existing relationships that still mean something to you. Rediscover the pleasures that you may now be taking for granted.

Be ready to help others. What you have gone through, survived, and surmounted has made you stronger. Others will suffer leavetaking. You can share your strength with them.

# *XXVII* MATURE DEPENDENCY

ONE OF THE FACTORS contributing to the increase in leave-taking trauma is acceptance of the proposition that maturity means lack of need for people.

The proposition is false. When we act on it we damage our lives. The mature person is not the person who can dispense with human relationships and exist entirely within himself. Real maturity calls for an understanding of our need for dependence, acceptance of appropriate degrees of dependence, and the structuring and maintenance of relationships to meet our changing needs in this area. We live healthy and productive lives with people, not without them. Commitment is necessary. This is the essence of maturity. And yet we tend to look at noncommitment as something to be desired.

The tied-down often envy the fancy-free. We make a hero of the wanderer. Wanderers form no close ties. They are always on the move. When they get bored they split and they jet. We see their images fixed on the cover of *People* magazine, but the people themselves are always on the move.

But there's a price tag on split chic. Take Jennifer.

You first see Jennifer at a party. She's hard to miss. She stands in a corner, drink in hand. People gravitate toward her —or rather, men gravitate toward her. She talks fast but stays cool. She is attractive, but that's only part of it. Her crisp aloofness seems to draw men. Her provocative frankness offers a kind of promise that incites a good many males to dream about its fulfillment. No matter how many people are around her, she seems always alone.

Jennifer was born to well-off parents living in an affluent suburb. Her father was a busy executive who traveled a lot. Her mother was involved in a wide variety of community activities. Jennifer spent a lot of time on her own.

Jennifer's parents were divorced when she was seven. She stayed with her mother, who married again after a year. That marriage ran into trouble almost from the start, and Jennifer's mother began to drink. The child was away at school for much of the time.

When Jennifer's mother died—Jennifer was twelve—the young girl felt nothing. She knew how she was supposed to act and she acted that way. When the pretense got to be too much she retired to her room, where she read.

Jennifer first had sex at fifteen. She wanted to try it. It did not seem like a big deal when it was over. She kind of liked the boy, but soon she was not seeing him any more. She had sex with quite a few boys in the next few years, although she never "went with" any boy for any length of time. Even so, Jennifer was not considered a pushover. There was always something too reserved, too hard about her. No matter how many times she went to bed, she was still a challenge for the boys.

Throughout this time Jennifer was technically living with her father, who had married again. Actually she saw even less of him than she had when she was a child. After she graduated and moved to New York she never saw him again.

Jennifer made it fast in business. The men around her were at first conscious only of her attractiveness and the aura of combined aloofness and availability that she projected. She slept with several of the men at the office, all of them well placed in the firm. After a while her male colleagues were saying that she was very bright and very tough "for a woman." Soon they stopped adding "for a woman."

At a convention Jennifer met the president of a competing firm. They had cocktails and dinner, but Jennifer turned down his bid to sleep with her. Within a month she had moved to his company in a much bigger job at considerably more money. She left her former company in a bad spot when she walked out on them.

The president of the new company assumed that he and Jennifer would culminate the relationship begun at the convention. He was disappointed. Coolly she turned him aside. His feelings were soothed by the dawning knowledge that he had recruited a woman of considerable talent. Jennifer's capability and capacity for handling intrigue made her a formidable rival for a lot of ambitious people. She more than held her own.

At twenty-five Jennifer got married. This surprised almost everyone who knew her—although no one could claim to know her very well. Andy, the man she married, was a thirty-year-old doctor with a lucrative practice in exurbia. She continued to work, taking relatively brief stretches of time to bear two children, a girl and a boy. From the start the children had the best of everything, although they did not see much of their mother.

Andy began to see less and less of his wife. He was still deeply in love with her, so he was shocked when she told him, six years after the marriage, that she wanted a divorce. What Jennifer wanted, Jennifer got. The settlement, plus

Jennifer's growing income, assured her plenty of money. She managed to keep custody of the children—Andy could not manage to get them—and they were soon away in expensive private schools.

Until this time Jennifer's numerous affairs had been casual, short-run alliances. Rick was a little different. She met him at a cocktail party. They found many things in common. Both were cool, bright, accomplished, successful, divorced, and were responsible for their children. From the first Jennifer enjoyed matching wits with Rick. They fenced with each other, using all of the razor-keen armament of two capable duelists. That they should go to bed together seemed utterly natural after the first five minutes. That they continued to see each other after a year, two years, was something of a surprise to Jennifer, perhaps to Rick too.

Jennifer had moved into an apartment in the city. Rick had his own apartment. They stayed with each other in each place as dictated by whim. Jennifer's children were usually away, as were Rick's. When the children were around, Rick and Jennifer made no effort to conceal the relationship.

At thirty-six Jennifer experienced her first real career setback. She had assumed that she would get the top job in her division of the company when it became available. The job opened up, but Jennifer did not get it. It went to a colleague who was widely known as a loyal, diligent worker and a nice person but who totally lacked Jennifer's brilliance and style. Jennifer decided that maybe she should move elsewhere. She thought getting another suitable job would be easy, but it was not. She had won a lot of respect in her industry but also a lot of enemies; many people were afraid of her, and she had no real friends. For the first time she felt that she would like to talk with somebody, really talk. But Rick brushed her off humorously, and there was no one else.

So Jennifer stayed at the company. Her brilliance did not diminish, but now there seemed to be more disposition to criticize her. This tendency was combined with a marked reduction in awe, particularly among younger people in the organization. Perhaps these factors contributed to the increased edge, amounting sometimes to near shrillness, in Jennifer's formidable verbal equipment.

Rick broke it off. He just said, "It's over, Jenny." Jennifer took it coolly—on the surface. Beneath, with Rick gone, she felt an unfamiliar emptiness. There was no shortage of men who wanted to sleep with her, and she slept with some of them. But no long-term connection followed, although this was not entirely at Jennifer's volition.

Now Jennifer is forty. The children, growing, have long since made their own lives. Jennifer is still attractive, brilliant, funny, capable. But now there is anxiety and tension. She wonders what is going to happen to her.

People who have control of their lives don't just wonder what will happen. They influence what happens. That is maturity. The psychological literature on the nature of maturity is voluminous. It boils down to six principles:

Accept yourself.

Accept others.

Keep your sense of humor.

Appreciate simple pleasures.

Enjoy the present.

Welcome work.

Begin the transition early. Examine your present state in terms of these principles, and enhance them in preparation for a smooth, painless and rewarding graduation into a fully satisfying phase of life.

*Accept yourself.* This is the most important principle of maturity and the hardest to achieve. You are on your way to maturity when you can appreciate yourself without trying to be what you cannot possibly be. The mature person appraises himself. He realizes that he has desirable traits as well as bad ones. Having resolved vital questions about his makeup, he stops fighting himself. He is able to turn his attention to the outside world.

Self-acceptance is a measure of emotional health as well as a way of building it. The self-accepting person is able to give up outgrown relationships without pain and to build new relationships without fear.

Your starting point is to know how you operate. Some spend agonizing hours of introspection, trying to probe into the deep recesses of their being. There is a simpler way. Look at what you *do;* what you do is, to a great extent, the reflection of what you are. Where are you strong, where are you weak? What do you like, what do you dislike? When you know these things about yourself you will know what you have to accept.

Be fair. Don't be overly hard on yourself, but don't give yourself a free ride either. It is just as bad to belittle one's superiorities as to overlook one's weaknesses. When you can accept and enjoy strengths, you know more about the kinds of relationships you need, and you won't suffer unduly from your defeats.

Distinguish between what can be changed (and should be changed) and what you will have to live with. Often this means distinguishing between attitude and behavior. For example, a person may be shy, uneasy at meeting new people. This might be an attitude that can't be changed. But that person may conclude that giving in to shyness altogether makes one a recluse and precludes the forming of new attachments. It will be necessary to *behave* in a way that makes it possible to meet and get along with people, even though the basic attitude may not vary much.

Somerset Maugham—a painfully shy person—became a superb writer and observer of human beings. Maugham attributed his success to his ability to recognize his defects. In *The Summing Up* he wrote: "I discovered my limitations and it seemed to me that the only sensible thing was to aim at what excellence I could *within them*. I knew that I had no lyrical quality. I had a small vocabulary, and no efforts that I could make to enlarge it much availed me. I had little gift of metaphor; the original and striking simile never occurred to me. Poetic flights and the great imaginative sweep were beyond my powers ... I was tired of trying to do what did not come easily to me.

"On the other hand, I had an acute power of observation and it seemed to me that I could see a great many things that other people missed. I could put down in clear terms what I saw. I had a logical sense, and if no great feeling for the richness and strangeness of words, at all events a lively appreciation of their sound. I knew that I should never write as well as I could wish, but I thought with pains *I could arrive at writing as well as my natural defects allowed.*"

A stranger to Maugham's work might think that some of this is false modesty. No. Maugham's writing does not soar into flights of fancy. His vocabularly is small and simple. He used these "weaknesses" to make himself a master of brevity and impact.

If you're like most people, these are the realities that you will find it hardest to accept about yourself:

You have had failures because of your own deficiencies.

You are not content with the place you now occupy in the world.

There are some situations in life that you handle awkwardly.

You have adolescent dreams that you have not given up.

There are some things about you that you would like to change but that you will never be able to change.

You grow as you accept your shortcomings. St. Augustine said: "We make a ladder of our vices, if we trample those same vices underfoot." And Martin Buber said: "Every man's foremost task is the actualization of his unique, unprecedented and never-recurring potentialities, and not the repetition of something that another, even the greatest, has already achieved.

*Accept others.* When you can accept yourself with all of your faults, you can accept others. You have to be able to do this if you are to form new relationships to replace the old. Often it is more difficult to accept the superiorities of others than their shortcomings.

Your relations with others are a basic test of your maturity. The way you react to their weaknesses, their laziness, their hostility—or to their effectiveness, their success, their good fortune—is not a judgment on them but on yourself.

If you react badly to someone else's deficiency, it's important to recognize why you do so. Don't kid yourself that you get angry because of his lack of logic. ("He's so stupid he drives me out of my mind!") If logic were the only thing involved, you would respond with logic, not with emotion. The real reason for your anger may be that you see his faults as a threat to you because it makes you doubt yourself. Your own insecurity has been aroused.

To accept others does not mean yielding to their follies. On the contrary, it is simply an admission of the basic truth (on which we unfortunately do not always act) that nobody is perfect. Accepting others enables you to recognize and handle their failings. You can oppose their errors without guilt because you know in your heart you have no desire to injure them.

Other-acceptance is vital to positive leavetaking, to the building of any new relationship involving people. When you accept others, you have the right to expect them to accept you, with all your own strengths and weaknesses. You don't have to give in to their whims, or pretend to be what you are not, in order to win their approval. A mature person does not need the approval of others to respect himself. Secure in his own self-respect, he forms relationships to satisfy his other needs.

When you accept others you stop being frightened at the

idea of depending on others. It has always been true that "no man is an island, entire of itself." It is particularly valid today. We must depend on others. Defensive attitudes toward dependency can damage one's entire approach to leavetaking, making the individual morbidly afraid to break off relationships and equally fearful of forming new ones.

We need others, not because they can do things for us, or because they are innately superior, but just because they are *others*. It is our nature. Once we admit that, we are on the way to forming attachments without anxiety or guilt. And we can break off attachments, when necessary, without fear or clinging.

Of course it's important to avoid overdependency. Here are some standards you can use to maintain your necessary dependencies on a healthy level.

*Dependency is occasional, not full-time.* The mature person forms far more associations than dependencies. An association is a bond between people, a relationship that offers mutual companionship, pleasure and satisfaction. The give/take ratio will vary, but on balance it comes out about even. Dependency is leaning on others. In times of real stress we need to lean on others. If we have formed healthy relationships, we can do this without guilt or fear, because we know that we, in turn, offer others the opportunity to depend on us when they are in need. The mature person consciously invites the aid of others to compensate for his weaknesses in moments of pressure; but this is not his permanent way of life. He remains independent in the area of his strengths, and he works on his weaknesses to lessen the need for dependency, while admitting that he can never get along without help in all respects. Conversely, the mature individual does not invite the dependency of others to fulfill his own needs.

*Mature dependency is realistic.* It is selective. It is directed only toward those who are willing and able to meet our needs. If either of these two conditions are not met, a realistic individual looks elsewhere for help. He does not feel rejected or frustrated.

*Mature dependency is reciprocal.* The traffic moves both ways. The well-adjusted individual can be depended on for help, understanding and sympathy when it is asked of him. He does not grudge it.

In a close relationship involving mutual dependency the give/take ratio oscillates. Each individual is at times a giver, at times a taker. There are long stretches when neither is dependent on the other; they associate, not out of need for help but because the association provides other satisfactions. The relationship is not maintained solely because one person thinks he is going to need the help of the other.

In such an association the balance sheet shows a profit for both parties.

*Mature dependency includes openness.* A healthy dependency often rests on a confidential relationship. One individual can say what he really thinks and feels to another without fear of misunderstanding or censure.

Sharing attitudes lets us unload feelings which, if bottled up, can fester and grow out of proportion. There is another benefit. When someone is confidential with you, the sharing helps you to get out of the rut of your own thinking and see things more broadly and objectively. Often when you are being most helpful to another, you are at the same time helping yourself.

The mature person is not indiscriminately confidential. He is choosy. Weak and immature people thrust their confidences on unwilling people, who are embarrassed by the unwanted burden. In a healthy network of relationships there are some with whom we maintain associations that remain superficial; we are friendly but casual. With others we may discuss some feelings, say about the job. To a few we confide our inmost thoughts.

All kinds of human bonds are necessary. Examine your own network of relationships. Is it balanced? Are there gradations? Do you have a satisfactory number of acquaintances with whom you spend time in a friendly fashion, a lesser number with whom you are more intimate, and a few—or even just one—with whom you can be really honest?

*Keep your sense of humor.* A sense of humor does not mean the ability to make people laugh. It is the capacity to see things—including, most important, oneself—in balance, and to smile at the episodes of life that are not serious.

A mature sense of humor is not exercised at the expense of others. The person who specializes in the cutting remark has not matured. He is in trouble. The pointed zingers he gets off are a cover for his own feelings of inadequacy.

Humor is one of the lubricants that make relationships work smoothly. In this respect it is important to successful leavetaking, because it helps us to break off the old tactfully and move into the new with grace. It is most valuable as a self-governing device that assists us to look at ourselves and the world around us without self-pity.

*Appreciate simple pleasures.* For some, life is a series of "fixes." They demand a succession of new and more jolting experiences. They seek ever-larger thrills. And they are inevitably frustrated. Life does not consist of never-ending stimulants. It is not formed of Big Occasions. Even if it were, the novelty and effect would soon wear off, as it does with drugs, and we would be driven on in the futile search for the ultimate thrill.

This is the "total orgasm" approach to life. Those who adopt it are always trapped in a flurry of messy leavetakings. They go into new associations looking for transcendental ecstasy. They are disappointed; so they move on and farther out.

The mature individual derives kicks from the commonplace, because the bulk of any association consists of commonplaces. Some like to walk in the woods; some like to go to the ball game; some find real excitement in reading books.

Repetition is anathema to people who cannot form mature associations. The second time something happens they are bored. They rationalize their immaturity by bestowing upon themselves the mantle of superior sensitivity. We hear some people talk about their boredom in terms that are ostensibly rueful but actually boastful. They are really saying, "See what a lot it takes to satisfy me. That makes me better than you."

In forming a new relationship the healthy individual expects the commonplace. He anticipates repetition. Satisfaction is a steady state, not an artificial euphoria sustained by a series of injections of novelty.

*Enjoy the present.* The mature person does not mortgage his psyche to an uncertain future. He knows how to make the most of today. He remembers yesterday and plans for tomorrow, but he lives in the present.

Monsignor William T. Greene of St. Patrick's Cathedral in New York once observed that each day should be lived as if it were "all time and eternity." This view kills morbid regret over the past and morbid worry over the future.

Immature people also have a great fear of tomorrow. They abhor leavetaking because it projects them into the unknown, and to them the unknown is always bad news. In psychological terms, they have a low tolerance for ambiguity.

As we take leave of outlived relationships, we necessarily move into areas of ambiguity. Maturity enables us to do so with confidence.

*Welcome work.* We all work. To people who have not achieved healthy balance, work is drudgery. The emotionally sound person knows how to enjoy the experience of doing work and the satisfaction of accomplishing. This is characteristic of the teacher, the writer, the mason, the cook. Thorstein Veblen spoke of the "instinct for workmanship" that should invest our days.

The person who cannot find a solid resource of support in

his occupation is severely handicapped in handling the transitions of life. He never finds the satisfaction referred to by Oliver Wendell Holmes: "To hammer out as compact and solid a piece of work as one can, to try to make it first rate." This is the goal of mature people.

# *XXVIII*  GO OR STAY?

THE DOMINANT IMPULSE today is toward leavetaking. We are impelled by outside pressures and inner forces to break existing relationships and seek new ones. There seems to have been a lot of work done on the road of life. Most of the old stoplights have been removed. Life stretches before us, a four-lane highway, down which we can breeze from one attachment to another. Do you feel as if you're in a rut, that not much is happening? Split! Get a new mate, new friends. Move to another job, a different place. What's stopping you?

The pendulum has swung through a wide arc. Once there were all kinds of considerations that made major leavetaking an awesome step. For one thing, the opportunities were not there. Few of us were rich enough or mobile enough to pull up stakes and move on.

Society frowned on leavetaking. We made our beds and we had to lie in them. Respectable married people did not break up. They stayed together, however unhappily, for the sake of the children, or for fear of what people would say, or to avoid harm to the husband's career. In the early 1960s Nelson Rockefeller appeared to have a clear shot at the Republican nomination for President and an excellent chance of election. His separation, divorce and remarriage were crippling setbacks. Today these considerations do not apply to politicians or to anybody else.

Now leavetaking makes one a member of the crowd rather than an exception. One of the spectacular media events of 1977 was Margaret Trudeau's separation from her husband, the Prime Minister of Canada, leaving him with custody of their three children. Mrs. Trudeau said, "I'll miss the children, but I don't have to be a twenty-four-hour mother. In fact, Pierre is a better parent." Rubin Todres of the University of Toronto, a leading Canadian sociologist, declared that this separation could lead to a surge of wifely desertions across Canada. He characterized the runaway wife as "an increasing North American phenomenon," and emphasized the likelihood that many wives would follow the lead of Mrs. Trudeau.

It is the nature of life today that mass impulses spring into life with astounding speed. A pervading societal pressure on women leads toward rejection of the concept of the "twenty-four-hour mother." Leavetaking (in this case, of the traditional housewife/mother role) is the thing to do. And in the absence of counteracting forces, more extreme leavetaking becomes increasingly the norm.

Mass movements foster opposing movements. So, in reaction to the spread of the idea that it is good to be a working mother, we now see such developments as the Martha Movement, named after the biblical person who was gently chided by Jesus for remaining a homebody rather than getting out into the world as her sister Mary had done (Luke 10:38–42). The Martha Movement, busily attracting dues-paying mem-

bers, states that its purpose is "to reaffirm the value of home-
making as a form of lifework, and to offer the nation's home-
makers an organizational home."

The statement contains considerable psychological validity.
These days we seem to need organizational, or at least societal,
underpinning for many of the important decisions of life. It
is not enough to decide that something is right for us; we
look around to find out who else is doing it and how many
of them there are.

Such things as the Martha Movement offer organized con-
sent and support for a way of life. This particular development
would seem to have a useful place, positioned somewhere between the more militant feminist movement and the "total
woman" concept which suggests that the wife turn her home
into a kind of domestic massage parlor.

The problem is that we are witnessing a marked accelera-
tion of the tendency to make life decisions—leavetaking decisions—predominantly on the basis of mass movements and
peer pressure rather than in terms of what is right for the
individual. When confronted with the possibility of a break
with accustomed relationships and values, it is all-important
for a person to evaluate the factors and make decisions in an
individual way. Mass movements should serve as informational
and supportive resources, not dominant influencing factors.
The decision to maintain or break a relationship ought to be
an individual one.

Peer pressure is hard to resist. In the old days the burden
of proof rested on the leavetaker. The man who moved from
company to company was a "job-hopper"; he had to justify
his mobility to a potential employer. Now people plan their
careers in terms of moving from job to job. Once the mother
who went out and worked had to have a compelling reason
for doing so or she would feel the disapproval of her contemporaries. Now she feels obliged to explain why she *doesn't*
have a paying job. A woman in New Haven, Connecticut,

when asked at parties, "What do you do?" replies, "I am a housekeeper for a Yale professor and tutor to his children." At first people murmur in approving wonderment; when they find out she is married to the man, they lose interest.

The outside factors impelling us toward leavetaking are joined by drives from within. Nowadays many of us are prey to the "last chance" reaction. We are driven to get out of the rut; break off associations; find new ways of life before it's too late; do something different. We follow the impulse and then cling desperately to our choice, though it may be a bad one.

A woman writes to Ann Landers (New York *Daily News,* December 1, 1976) that her husband quit "a wonderful job to open up a radio and TV repair shop in our basement." The man has painted the house red and put up a garish sign on the porch. The phone rings constantly. There is no privacy. Their daughter has moved out. Fuses blow all the time. And the husband is losing all their savings. The man's boss has called three times to ask him to return to his old job. No; he prefers being self-employed.

Ann Landers advises the woman to give her husband ten days to go back to his job; otherwise she should move out.

It happens. People take leave of a stage of life because they feel that life is passing them by, and if they don't act their world will take leave of them. The phase they move into turns out to be thoroughly unsatisfactory. Nevertheless they cling to the new association. They are like survivors of a sunken ship, hanging on to the last bit of flotsam. The new situation, bad as it is, is their last chance.

The last-chance reaction is a dangerous possibility when a person undertakes what he thinks is a voluntary leavetaking under emotional circumstances that do not permit him to consider the situation objectively. The parting is really forced, by frustration, by anger, by a sense of time passing. If it were clearly forced by outside circumstances, the individual would not feel totally committed to it. But since he feels that he has done it entirely on his own, he sticks to his purpose with stubborn intensity in a manner that is destructive of others and of himself.

When one makes this sort of emotional break with the past, the road back often remains open for a time. The boss would like you back; the abandoned partner would welcome your return. But to go back is the one option that you will not consider.

The key to this situation is understanding the difference between a partial leavetaking and a complete one. People who feel "stuck" are frequently well advised to undertake a trial venture into another mode of life while retaining the framework of the previous associational network. If the new departure doesn't work out, they can go back.

The impulsive break with the past is not a deliberate effort at partial leavetaking, but it can have the effect of one. If this is the case, then the leavetaker should acknowledge it, and admit to himself that he is lucky enough to be able to retrace his steps if that is the right thing to do.

He is held back from doing so by pride and guilt. He is too proud to admit a mistake. He feels guilty about the pain his action has given to others. He is determined to prove that he was right. Illogically, his determination feeds on failure. This is supposedly his last chance—at money, independence, at pleasure, at *life.* So he plays it out to the end, averting his eyes from the evidence that it has gone sour.

If the new association were truly the last chance, there might be some justification for doing this. But that is rarely the case. The last-chance problem exists in the mind of the leavetaker.

When going back is possible, it should be considered along with all other options. It is not as if the abandoned venture must be written off as a complete waste. It is experience, and experience is not wasted. The person who has, on his own, cast aside existing involvements to try new ones has learned something about a different way of living. It may be that at some time in the future he will want to try something similar again. Next time he will know what mistakes to avoid and be conscious of the need for considering carefully all of the factors in his contemplated actions and all of their possible consequences. He will, too, appreciate the luxury of being able to decide his own fate rather than having it decided for him by time, circumstances and other people.

Moreover, the person who fails in a new relationship and backtracks into the old will have given himself the chance to appreciate the prior ties. He now knows what he valued most in the past involvement. True, he knows also the things that made him unhappy. But now he has an opportunity to do something to set these things to rights.

An impulsive and doomed leavetaking need not be a disaster. What can make it disastrous is inflexible insistence on pursuing a course that leads directly to calamity. Victims of the last-chance reaction are peculiarly victims of themselves.

The last-chance syndrome sets in at a time of major leavetaking. The individual reacts as if this were the final opportunity to realize fulfillment. When one important association is broken, all associations are categorized as restrictive and unsatisfying. "Now," the person says, "is my last chance to grab for all the 'gusto.'" After all, he reasons, the commercials tell us that we only go around once in life and we must go all out for all the pleasure we can get.

In many ways leavetaking is seen as the alchemist's stone that will enable us to turn back the clock. Movement is the way to stay young. We become thralls to the illusion of reversibility.

One of the principal concomitants of the illusion of reversibility is rage. We grow older; we think that it does not have to happen; we are angry at ourselves for permitting it to happen. And we get angry at those around us, particularly those who are younger or those who appear to have found the secret of staying young. We hear more and more about the "anger of the middle-aged man." Books are written about the plight of males who have been rejected by the industrial system that nurtured them for so long. True, we seem to have adopted a cult of youth; and central to this cult is the idea that youth can be maintained indefinitely or resumed if only we read the right books, buy the right products, wear the right clothes, and in all respects work at being young.

Thus in print and on TV we have a new hero, the middle-aged man who drops out, who pulls out of the rat race and does his thing. His thing invariably involves the aping of life styles of people who are twenty or thirty years his juniors. Dropping out is thought to be synonymous with a successful reversion to youth. The middle-aged person who is trying to do what Canute could not do adopts "young" styles in speech, dress, hair and behavior. Responsibility is a taint of age; it cannot be tolerated. The shucking off of responsibility becomes an ideal.

The attempt to turn back the clock is a denial of all of the things we are and could be, and an impossible quest for the one thing that we absolutely cannot have.

The initial effect of jettisoning all existing relationships can be one of lightheadedness, almost of euphoria. We are *free*. But free for what? Contrary to the message of the advertisements, the paramount good is not to grab for all the gusto you can get, as if life were a carousel that takes only one turn and affords only one shot at the brass ring. Life is more cyclical than that. There are brass rings of varying sizes and qualities. The object is healthy growth, not spasmodic efforts to seek pleasure.

Extreme leavetaking is not in itself a positive good, however it may be endorsed by current opinion. When events precipitate a severe break in one's life, there is always the possibility of making the break more sweeping than it has to be. This is the proper course if indeed this particular rupture has broken the logjam of a mass of unsatisfactory relationships that were keeping the individual from self-fulfillment. But if the still-existing relationships are healthy and satisfactory ones, their abandonment will result in greater misery.

When you are confronted with a severe leavetaking, it is wise to use the occasion to examine each of your associations on its own merits. The fact that a husband-wife relationship has gone sour does not mean that one's bonds with children, friends, occupation and community are equally bad and unnecessary. On the contrary, this may be the time to renew and revitalize those associations that do provide a positive psychic payout and that may be all the more important now.

Separate and identify each association. Consider its pluses and minuses—its income-outgo ratios—separated, as far as is possible, from concurrent associations. Obviously your associations overlap. You cannot isolate them altogether. The important thing is to offset the lumping-together tendency that will impel you toward abandoning the good along with the bad, and going farther in trying to erase the past than you have to go or than you should go. The cliché "Don't throw the baby out with the bath water" is particularly appropriate in considering what happens to the children when a marriage breaks up.

Once you are at the point of examining your relationships from a positive point of view, there is no need to rush things. Should you decide that a completely new way of life is the right course for you, you can move toward it. It is difficult and often impossible to repair breaks that have been made finally but too hastily.

Whatever answer you find, it must be *your* answer, correct and satisfying for you. New departures that are undertaken at the urging of friends or through the influence of mass movements are apt to be thorough but unhappy.

Leavetaking is not an intrinsic good. Neither is nonleavetaking of itself a praiseworthy or desirable course of action. To sever relationships for trivial reasons, or because everybody else is doing it, is the opposite of a guarantee of happiness. To remain in artificial togetherness because of fear or unhappy experience is equally unfulfilling.

Leavetaking is a part of life and a concomitant of growth, but this does not make indiscriminate or clumsy breaking of associations a worthwhile thing.

The essence of successful handling of leavetaking is *decision.* Whether we decide to go or to stay, the decision must be based on valid factors and objective thought. The choice of a course of action must rise from the knowledgeable center of the self.

When we understand the nature and importance of leavetaking, perceive our vulnerability to its various manifestations, and develop strategies to deal with it, we enhance our chances of healthy growth through successive stages of satisfying maturity.

# Index

279